MY DIARY
August 30th to November 5th, 1874

Cornelia Adair

My Diary

AUGUST 30TH TO NOVEMBER 5TH, 1874

by Cornelia Adair

Introduction by Montagu K. Brown

Illustrations by Malcolm Thurgood

UNIVERSITY OF TEXAS PRESS, AUSTIN & LONDON

Library of Congress Catalog Card No. 65–11153
Copyright © 1965 University of Texas Press
All rights reserved
Printed by the University of Texas Printing Division, Austin
Bound by Universal Bookbindery, Inc., San Antonio

PUBLISHER'S FOREWORD

Montagu Kingsmill Brown, a young Britisher just out of the Boer War, arrived at the new town of Pampa in the Texas Panhandle in 1903 and there found a home which satisfied fully his restless ambition and fitted perfectly his exuberant outlook on life. When he died sixty-one years later there was scarcely an important institution or civic enterprise in the area which had not gained vitality both from his financial support and from his strikingly individualistic participation and leadership. Typical of his activities was a personal and completely unpublicized philanthropy: each year he selected and sent to college several young men and women of promise whose formal education would otherwise have ended. His influence will continue through the foundation which bears his name and through his wise and selective investments in people. Few men have left a more constructive impress upon a region.

"Texas has been very good to me," M. K. Brown said. "I want to repay my debt to it in every way I can."

In 1960, Mr. Brown made another substantial payment on his debt to Texas through a gift to the University of Texas Press establishing the M. K. Brown Range Life Series. Through this series he and the Press hoped to record in depth the experiences of Mr. Brown's fellow pioneers of the Southwest, particularly in the Panhandle. Five important books had been published in this series before M. K. Brown died in an automobile accident in 1964. The series will be continued.

72130

Shortly before his death Mr. Brown suggested to the Press that it publish a new edition of *My Diary* by Cornelia Wadsworth (Mrs. John) Adair, an extremely rare piece of Western Americana. It was as Assistant Manager of the Adair's famed JA ranch that Montie Brown spent some of his most satisfying years. Mr. Brown said that he did not want *My Diary* to appear as a part of his Range Life Series because it didn't really fit, but that he wanted to made a special gift to the Press to enable its publication as a personal tribute to "a very great lady."

M. K. Brown hadn't finished the final draft of his introduction to *My Diary* when his life was cut tragically short, but he had done enough on it to enable his friend, Mrs. Clotille Thompson, to complete the job. The Press owes particular gratitude to her, to Mrs. Iris Ragsdale, and to Mrs. Mary Ann McCloskey for their assistance. Thanks are also due to Wm. Jarrell Smith and the M. K. Brown Foundation for fulfilling Mr. Brown's commitment and making possible the publication of this book.

The copy of the original edition used in the preparation of this book was presented to M. K. Brown by Mrs. Adair with the following inscription:

M K Brown, from his friend Cornelia Adair March 1920.

Montagu K. Brown

INTRODUCTION

It is a privilege to know a great person. And perhaps an even greater privilege to be able to tell others about such a person. Thus I consider it an honor and privilege to share a friendship and pay tribute to a very fine lady by producing this little *Diary* of Mrs. Adair's, which she kept while on a buffalo hunting trip into this western country with her husband, John Adair.

My acquaintance with Mrs. Adair came about many years after this trip was made, when she, as owner of the JA Ranch was advised by a friend, Vere Finch, who had land adjoining the JA, to hire Mr. T. D. Hobart as ranch manager for the JA. At this time I was assistant to Mr. Hobart, who was manager of White Deer Lands. It seems that Mrs. Adair's nephew James W. Wadsworth, Jr., who had been managing the Ranch for a number of years, was called back to New York by his colleagues there to run for the United States Senate from the State of New York. He had done an excellent job of running the Ranch and Mrs. Adair was anxious to acquire another manager of like caliber. After visiting with Mrs. Adair at the Ranch, Mr. Hobart agreed to take the job provided it met with the approval of his employers, the English proprietors of the White Deer Lands under the trusteeship of Frederic de

Peyster Foster. And there was one other stipulation. He asked that he be allowed to bring along M. K. Brown as his assistant. This was a lucky day for me! Mrs. Adair agreed and promptly invited me down to the Ranch for a visit. I could not go at that particular time, and later when I was available, she had returned to England on one of her annual visits. And so I did not actually meet her until some two or three years later.

But wait a bit—before I go on with this part of the story, I must first tell you something of the background and early life of Mrs. Adair, in order to give you a clearer picture of what a remarkable lady she really was.

Mrs. Adair was born Cornelia Wadsworth, whose family pioneered the Geneseo Valley of New York in the middle and late 1700's. They built fabulous houses, The Homestead and Hartford House, which remain to this day, and in which the Wadsworth descendants still live. The Wadsworth name is still well known in high government places. Stuart Symington of Missouri married a niece of Mrs. Adair; and her nephew who managed the Ranch had a son, Ambassador James J. Wadsworth, who I believe was a United States representative on the Disarmament Commission of the United Nations, and has held other high government offices.

But to get back to the early-day Wadsworths. Mrs. Adair told me numerous stories of exciting and tremendously funny experiences of her forbears. This side of their life seemed to interest her as much as, if not more than, the fact that they were a family of social prominence who had a great deal to do with our early history.

General Jeremiah Wadsworth served with Washington dur-

Mrs. Adair and JA ranch workers. The five men directly behind Mrs. Adair are (from left to right) Whitfield Carhart, K. W. Kent (range superintendent), T. D. Hobart (manager), M. K. Brown (assistant manager), Henry Rowden (straw boss)

ing the Revolution. And it was Captain Joseph Wadsworth, a great-uncle of Mrs. Adair, who snatched the Connecticut Charter from under the very nose of the Royal Governor, thus committing the first act of rebellion by the colonists against the British Crown. Though Joseph never actually admitted to doing this, he was later voted a sum of money by the Council of Connecticut for safeguarding and preserving the document. It had been hidden in the trunk of a great oak tree, which was known thereafter as the Charter Oak. This fact is recorded in our history books, but I was privileged to hear about it from one of the direct descendants of the very chap who was able to pull off this neat trick. I'd like to have known this Captain Joe myself. He wasn't afraid of a fight. He was my kind of folks, and could have easily been a Texan, except for a slight accident of birthplace.

But to get on with the story. It seems that General Jeremiah Wadsworth, who lived at the time in Connecticut, had acquired land in the Geneseo Valley of New York and was anxious to see the land developed; he sold a vast tract to two of his nephews, James and William. Both brothers possessed tremendous ability and energy, and together they founded in this place the ancestral home of this great family. James fought in the Revolutionary War and was a member of the Continental Congress from 1783 to 1786. His son, James Samuel, was the father of Mrs. Adair. He was a general in the Union Army during the Civil War, and finally lost his life in the battle of the Wilderness. His son Craig (brother of Mrs. Adair) was General Sheridan's aide, and she speaks of this relationship in her diary. This probably accounts for the personal interest General Sheridan took in providing an escort for the buffalo hunt which is described in the Diary.

Mrs. Adair enjoyed relating these stories, especially those concerning her father's early escapades. She said he was probably the "spoiled brat" of his family, which consisted of five children. He led a rather colorful life, to say the least, during his growing-up period, and was even expelled from Harvard. No one ever knew exactly why, but the story that came down through the family was that it was for "disciplinary infraction," which, as Mrs. Adair said, at Harvard usually meant alcohol or women, and her father was not known for his excessive drinking.

At any rate he'd had his taste of life and was ready to settle down when he met and fell in love with Mary Craig Wharton, probably the most beauteous of all the beautiful Wadsworth women. They were married, and built a home in the Geneseo Valley—copied from a villa in England—which they called Hartford House. They were very near to the original family home, The Homestead, and in the years that followed they increased the Clan by six. The author of this Diary was the second of their six children.

James Samuel Wadsworth, like his father, loved the British aristocratic way of life, and after the Hartford House was completed, he set about creating in this valley of his a "Little England." Thus it was that Cornelia grew up in an atmosphere completely foreign to this cattle country of the Panhandle of Texas, yet her spirit and broad vision were as truly Western as if she had lived here her entire life. She was an all round good scout and a real Queen of the Cattle Country.

Mrs. Adair and Colonel Charles Goodnight (1917)

Her first marriage, in 1857, was to Montgomery Ritchie of Boston, a grandson of Harrison Otis. He died in 1864 of an illness resulting from his years of service in the Civil War. Their son, Monty Ritchie, still lives at least a part of the time I think, on what is left of the original JA Ranch. A few years later, while attending a ball in New York in the home of Congressman J. C. Hughes, who was a friend of the Wadsworth family, she met John Adair, who was also at the ball. A couple of years later, in 1869, she and Adair were married, and he took her to visit his vast estates in England and Ireland on their honeymoon trip. One of these estates she told me contained a residence and 27,000 acres of grazing land—very rough country. Adair also owned property on the coast near the town of Rathdaire, on which was located a beautiful home and where they spent a good deal of time. This place was a favorite of hers, and when Adair died this is where he was buried.

It was about the year 1876 that their travels took them out to Denver, where they met Colonel Charles Goodnight, a trailblazer and Indian scout. Goodnight was contemplating the purchase of several thousand acres of ranch land in the Palo Duro Canyon. This comprised the counties of Armstrong, Briscoe, Donley, Hall, Randall, and Swisher. The State of Texas had given alternate sections of land for school land, and the patented sections were then allocated to settlers. The story goes that in surveying the land, the surveyors came up with some mighty "trail-windy" section lines in order that the choice sections (those with water on them) would go to certain people. Word of this leaked out somehow, and the system of allocating was reversed, which just naturally loused up the whole scheme. Colonel Goodnight had picked out the Palo Duro area because he felt it would be excellent for grazing, and for protecting cattle during the brisk blizzards of those early-day winters. (Those people who think we have blizzards nowadays are just too soft for my craw. They should have lived here when we had blizzards that had character. These present-day civilized little blows that radio and TV get so worked up about are only good for stirring up tired blood and keeping the circulation going. Shoot! Why I can remember—well—that's another story. I will probably get around to telling it in my own book, which I am now working on.) Back to the Adairs—

Colonel Goodnight and John Adair formed a partnership and established the JA Ranch, operating it together until Adair's death. Mrs. Adair then purchased Goodnight's interest and continued to operate the Ranch and to visit it regularly. Her manager, prior to her nephew James W. Wadsworth, Jr., was an Irishman by the name of Dick Walsh, who ran the Ranch for many years until his marriage to the daughter of an Episcopal bishop from Toronto, Canada. Mrs. Walsh did not fit into the picture in the management of the Ranch in Texas, so Mr. Walsh finally resigned, and Mrs. Adair, out of the goodness of her heart, prevailed upon some of her very influential friends in England to obtain for him the position of manager of the British government's ranches in Rhodesia. He later died there and was buried in Bulawayo, Southern Rhodesia.

It was then that she asked her nephew to come and manage the Ranch for her, which he did for about four years. He, like

PHOTOGRAPH BY ERWIN E. SMITH

Breakfast at 4 A.M. on the JA

his aunt, was well liked by everyone he met. Though an East-
erner brought up in great wealth, he rode with the cowboys,
knew as much as any of them about cattle and horses, and was
completely fair and honest in all his dealings. He had the respect of everyone with whom he worked and was having quite
a good time of it himself when he was called back to New
York as I mentioned earlier.

Since the death of John Adair, Mrs. Adair had made a practice of coming from her home, which she now made in England, to Texas via New York each fall. I believe it was the year
1917 when we were preparing for her visit to the Ranch that
I suggested to Mr. Hobart that we meet her at Memphis on the
Fort Worth and Denver Railroad and escort her on to Clarendon, Texas, where she maintained a lovely residence in the City
of Clarendon, as well as at her Headquarters on the JA Ranch
at Palo Duro. This we did, and it was a very pleasant occasion.
On this trip she was, as usual accompanied by her private secretary, Miss Joan Royse, her personal maid, one cook, and one
housemaid, all from England.

It was her practice to visit the Headquarters and look over
the cattle and ranch land which, at that time, numbered some
500,000 acres of land, 30,000 head of cattle, and 700 horses.
She got a real thrill out of these trips, and in the course of the
years that followed I had occasion to make the arrangements
for many more such trips.

One in particular I remember because it was probably the
last visit she paid to her old home in Geneseo. She was accompanied by a very dear friend, the Countess of Dartry and her
personal maid. They came by steamer and landed in New

Roundup on the JA

Cowboy and dogs on the JA

York. Mrs. Adair had requested that I go east to New York and make all the necessary arrangements for their trip, which I did. However, I did not meet them in New York, but in Buffalo, where we spent several delightful days sightseeing. I had learned that Mrs. Adair's nephew was now up for re-election to the Senate, and was making a political speech in Buffalo; so I took the ladies to hear the speech.

Lady Dartry also wanted to visit a friend of hers, her former personal maid in England, who was now living in this area. We all went to pay her a call, and found that even though she had lived within thirty miles of Niagara Falls for many, many years, she had never seen the Falls; whereupon we took her with us to view this wondrous spectacle. This seems to be typical of people living near world-famous places. They are the ones who never get around to seeing them while others come from half way round the world to see these things. (I know this to be true of my brother Eustace, who, at the age of 84 and still residing in London, has not as yet visited the Houses of Parliament; unless he has done so in very recent years without my knowledge.)

Mrs. Adair was a great contributor to many civic projects in the vicinity of her Ranch Headquarters. She built the hospital in Clarendon, Texas, which is still in existence and still bears the name Adair Hospital. She also built one of the early-day Y.M.C.A.'s in Clarendon, which has since been turned over to the City Dads and made into the City Hall.

She strongly supported the Episcopal Church in Clarendon, the Mother Church of the Panhandle. In addition she supported the Boy Scout movement, as she knew many of the original British organizers of that institution in England.

It was my privilege in the few years that I worked for her to make the arrangements for much of the entertainment of her friends and illustrious relatives from New York and England. After learning that her son and I were in the same regiment during the Boer War in Africa, Mrs. Adair insisted that I give her secretary the name and address of my mother, and on one of her trips back to England she entertained both my mother and two of my sisters in her home in London, at 11 Portman Square.

The time came when Mrs. Adair felt that she owned too much land and that it should be distributed among other landowners and cattle ranchers, and she suggested that Mr. Hobart and I offer some of her land for sale. She was always quite interested in knowing just who was buying the land, and I suggested to her that it would be good business to meet some of the cattlemen and landowners who purchased cattle and vast areas of land from her. She agreed, and asked me to make arrangements for her to invite the gentlemen and their wives to her Ranch Headquarters at Palo Duro. This was accomplished and she enjoyed entertaining them, both at the Ranch and at her home in Clarendon. In fact, she enjoyed these personal meetings so much that she often wondered why this policy was not followed by everyone interested in selling land.

In thinking back about Mrs. Adair and the whole Wadsworth family, it is interesting to me to note that their interests touched every facet of life, yet they remained essentially a people of the land—farmers, dairymen, cattle raisers, and such. They delved into a multitude of business ventures and politics, always politics. Yet they never released their contact and kinship with the land.

And by gorry, I believe there is something to be learned from this observation. I'm going to think about it for a good while tomorrow morning over my second cup of coffee— about 6:00 A.M. That's when I do my best thinking and make my best plans.

MONTAGU K. BROWN

PREFACE

I have had this old diary of mine printed because I thought it would be nice for my grand-children and grand-nieces and nephews, and young friends generally, to have it. They will always remember me as an old lady who sat in an armchair, and whose stick had to be looked for; and how, when they came to see me, their mother or their nurse said, "Now, don't make too much noise." But not so many years ago I was a very lively person, and when this diary was written I did all sorts of exciting things, as they will see.

Another reason why I have thought it worthwhile to have it printed is, that the world is changing so quickly, ways of travelling especially so (though in forty-four years I find that a Pullman Sleeping Car in the United States has changed less than most things!), and I think it may be interesting to compare what was done in 1874 with what will be done by the time the children are able to travel. No doubt they will do their journeys by air, and do many, many things that I have not been able to do; but they can never see the prairies of America in their wild uncivilised state, or hunt buffalo over them, nor can they pow-wow with the Red Indians in a camp on the Platte River. So every time has its own special joys, and the great thing is to miss as little as possible, and to share as much.

CONTENTS

ILLUSTRATIONS

MY DIARY
August 30th to November 5th, 1874

John Adair

Voyage in the S.S. Cuba

August 30th, 1874—We left Portarlington this morning, and ran down to Queenstown very comfortably in almost the only quick train in Ireland—the Sunday "American Mail," as it is called.

We found on the *Cuba's* tender some of our fellow-passengers—Mr. Blackmore, who we had heard was going out with us, and would be able to tell us a great deal about the West, and help us more than anybody in arranging our plans for seeing wild sport on the Prairies; Judge Parsons, a great railway magnate in America, and so clever and amusing, with any number of the raciest stories *à propos* of everything, only, as he told me to-day, so many of them had such a strong "Westerny" flavour, that he is afraid to tell them to "ears polite." Then there were Mrs. Stevens, of New York, and her lovely daughter—the "American beauty" who had half London at her feet last season, not alone for the *beaux yeux de sa cassette,* which some jealous spirits have affirmed—but, although her *cassette* is so much larger and more real than most of those one hears of, there are other heiresses in London, and, if she had not been so charming in every way and so thoroughly nice, London would not have been so unanimous as it was in her favour. I do think one may honestly say that to the credit of Society.

Of course, the arrangements at Queenstown for getting one's things and oneself on board the steamer are as troublesome and ill-contrived as possible. We found the same old lot of donkey-carts with wretched-looking ragged drivers waiting to impose on rich American travellers—but they have succeeded only too well—for now, everything being so uncomfortable, the only hotel so dirty and badly kept, the two stations (on the same line) at Cork, where you have to drive in a dirty inside car from one to the other and the nuisance of changing luggage, indeed, the difficulty of getting it safely carried at all from one station to the other, and twenty other annoyances, have quite stopped the stream of Americans who would be only too glad to shorten the sea voyage and see Ireland and open the eyes of the natives with their profuse liberality. It is such a pity that the Great Southern and Western Railway have so little enterprise and seem determined to make things as uncomfortable as possible for everybody.

The last half-hour I have passed settling myself in this tiny cabin. Every ledge and hook is occupied, everything is within reach and I am prepared for the worst. A slight roll, and a soupçon of a pitch, which is far worse than anything, tell me that we are getting out of the harbour. I ought to go up on deck and look at the Irish shore—that was a roll! I think I will wait until we return from America to see the Irish shore. The stewardess, delightfully fat and good-natured-looking with a pair of fine spectacles poised on the tip of her nose, has just come in and advises me strongly to "go to bed at once." "Oh, Stewardess, you do not think that it is going to be very rough soon, do you?" "All I can say, ma'am, is the sooner you get into that berth the happier you'll be."

September 5th—The worst was *very very* very terrible, and no one sympathises with me, excepting the faithful steward-ess. "Ah, Stewardess, I know I shall die. I shall never reach America alive!" "It *is dreadful,* my love, I am sure, but you won't die, my dear. Now take a drop of this nice champagne." She always called one "my love" and "my dear," which is rather soothing in sea-sickness. And through it all, the pitch-ing and tossing and rolling, those gossamer spectacles were always exactly in the same place, with her bright eyes peering over them. How she kept them there was a problem, and why she wanted them at all.

There is an Italian opera-troupe on board, and the tenor and baritone have a cabin very near this one. They have the most excited discussions at the top of their voices. The bari-tone has just informed the tenor that, if they are shut up much longer together, their bones will be all that is left. On deck they forget their squabbles and perform the most ridiculous antics. The baritone has a delicious sympathetic voice, and sometimes they sing (and make one long for more) for the amusement of the Prima Donna and one or two very yellow friends of hers, who sit together wrapped-up in all sorts of curious odds and ends, and give sickly little deprecating smiles at their jokes.

September 6th—We have been very busy to-day studying maps with Mr. Blackmore. He thinks our best chance of seeing sport is to try and get up a party from Fort Dodge. Colonel Dodge, who has been in command there lately, has several times organised the most delightful hunting parties—so well arranged that, although they were camping out for more than a fortnight, and never during that time communicating with their "base," they had every comfort: very nice tents with iron bedsteads, easy chairs, and even ice for their champagne. And he says I could go as well, and as comfortably as possible, if I do not mind long rides. This sounds charming, for I should not like being shut up for a fortnight in one of those Western forts, waiting for my belongings to return. The Judge has been giving us an alarming account of Western cookery: "The thin leathery fried beefsteaks—omelettes that you can take hold of by one end and fling across the street—bread, that if you throw a piece of it against the wall would stick there."

September 9th—I thought the worst was really over when I last wrote, we were sailing along so calmly day after day—new faces appearing every morning, the decks full of people walking up and down, and sitting out under the stars late every night, everybody cheery and pleasant, the two young Italians more full of tricks than ever. We had formed such a pleasant little coterie and relieved the dreadful ennui of the voyage by gay little suppers, enlivened by many of the Judge's good stories, and often by a song or duet which the Italians were kind enough to sing for us, not to speak of the wonderful and pretty tricks of legerdemain which Mr. Maddock gave for our amusement, and his charming songs, more suited for our small quarters almost than the powerful tremolo of the *tenore robusto*.

Yesterday we had a rude awakening. It was a day of intense discomfort: it began by blowing early in the morning—a dreadfully hot burning wind like a tremendous sirocco—after breakfast it had increased to such a gale and so suddenly that, before anyone suspected what was going to happen, two great waves broke over the ship, shivering a skylight and completely drenching everybody who was on deck. Every door and port-hole had to be fastened, and we were all shut up in the stifling heat in a sort of half-darkness—then began a scene of hustle and noise and confusion which lasted all day. Every instant great seas washed over the ship, dashing against her with such force that she shook and quivered under them, straining and creaking like a creature in agony. Every movable article was knocked about. The Italians were dreadfully frightened and miserable, screaming and praying; but the intense depressing heat was worse than anything.

With the greatest difficulty Miss S. and I got down to our cabins, where we abandoned ourselves to despair and the tender mercies of the stewardess. If I had not been so frightfully ill I think I should have enjoyed the excitement, and then the sea was so glorious to look upon, the sun shone brightly the whole day, giving colour and light and shade. Generally, in a storm everything is grey and dull, but this was all the most brilliant blue and green. Towards night it got quieter, and the next morning only a great surging swell remained. It was curious to see what the storm had done. The strong brass rail-

ing around the deck was bent like a wire. Some of the sails
were carried away, others torn literally into ribbons before
they had time to get them down. The jib-boom was snapped-
off like a stick, with three sailors clinging to it at the time.
They managed somehow to jump off, falling in a loose sail,
and were saved. Captain Martyn was in his element. The
stewardess, who has given me her opinion in confidence on
all the Captains and all the steamers of the Cunard Line, says
he is a "first-rate sailor and a great one to drive, and there is
not a ship on the ocean she'd sooner trust her children in than
the *Cuba,* though they do call her the creeping crawling *Cuba."*

The Pilot came on board to-day amid the usual scene of excitement and betting. The colour of his hair, whether he will
wear an overcoat, which leg he will first step on board with,
or whether he will have a moustache. For a day or two before
he is picked up all the smoking-room is absorbed in taking
the odds on these points, and talks of nothing else. It is a
change from the betting on the daily run, or the everlast-
ing games of poker and euchre. He brought with him the
last New York newspapers, with reports of Indian wars,
just where we were thinking of making our happy hunting-
grounds. Mr. Blackmore says we shall have to go farther
North. Our Italians are delighted with the flourishing accounts of themselves in the New York papers and are in great
good humour, embracing one another with effusion and sing-
ing duets and snatches of every sort of drinking-song and
bravura, much to the disgust of their impresario—Mr. Stra-
kosch, who is afraid they will injure their voices by exerting
them in the open air, and growls at them with little effect; in

fact, the *tenore robusto* defies him. "Mon organe c'est â moi" he declares, and shouts out *Di provenza il man* at the top of his voice and with such a tremolo that I am afraid the critical New Yorkers will not appreciate at all.

New York

September 10th—Arrived in New York this morning, after a long wait off Staten Island for the Health Officer, who did not hurry himself in coming on board. The day is very hot. Even in three years the town is so changed, such wonderful new buildings everywhere, but the same dirty ill-paved streets. One sees very quickly that one has arrived in a city governed by an Irish municipality! And the same weedy long-tailed horses and horrid old lumbering omnibuses crowding the best streets, such a contrast to the extraordinary lightness of all the other carriages. Our "hack" which brought us up from the steamer over the roughly-paved streets—filled with holes that would be thought almost impossible in an out-of-the-way

country road in England—with our heavy boxes piled up behind and on the driver's seat, had wheels and springs more
airy and delicate looking than the lightest London-made vic-
toria. The first and greatest novelty that struck me was the
aerial railroad[1] which runs through, or rather over, the streets
from one end of New York to the other. It gave one a start to
see a train of cars running over one's head on the lightest iron
framework and supported, or rather balanced, as it appears
to be, on a *single* line of iron columns down the centre. I confess I should prefer *terra firma,* and they say trains have tumbled over once or twice, but when I saw it the carriages were
full of people.

We were recommended to try the Brunswick Hotel, a new
house on Fifth Avenue, and we find it charming, though the
street is rather noisy. We have a very nice suite of rooms and
there is an excellent restaurant downstairs. All these new
hotels and many of the private houses have such pretty arrangements of tropical-looking plants in front of them, where
the area would be: beds and vases filled with palms, coleus
and creepers, making the gayest and most graceful effects.

Though the New-Yorkers are hardly yet supposed to have
returned from the seaside and country, it seems to me as if
there were as many pretty women in the streets as ever, and
looking so *chic* and well-dressed, almost all in black as is the
fashion here, but very slender and delicate. It is wonderful
how well-dressed they are, so quietly and in such good taste,
and I know that half of those one meets have their dresses

---

[1] These were the first elevated railways in New York, and have
since been replaced by more solid structures.

made at home—made by their own hands most likely—for
dressmakers here are so frightfully extravagant, and are such
expensive luxuries, that numbers of my countrywomen manage to do without them. The men, as usual, seem haggard and
anxious-looking, and all wear white hats with a black band.
The noise and clatter of the streets is so confusing, and my
head is very shaky with a distinct *Cuba* roll in it still. This day
seems a week long; it began at 2 this morning. Fancy being
aroused in one's first sleep by the "boots steward" thrusting
his lantern in at one side of the curtain across my door, turning the bull's-eye on to my berth and insisting upon my iden-
tifying my own boots from a lot in a basket which he held inside the cabin at the other side of the curtain, as he "had got
them mixed up!" It was very aggravating. Then, at 4, Captain
Gore came to wake us up, as we had "arrived" and, of course,
I should be dying with impatience to see my native land. But
we did not leave the ship until 10 o'clock.

September 11th—Last night we dined at Delmonico's with
Mr. Blackmore, and I had the pleasure of eating *fricassée* frog
for the first time—it was like tasteless chicken. All these
restaurants are crowded every evening just as in Paris, and
look very bright, lighting up the street with their numerous
brilliant gas-jets. They have the best French cooks, and towards 6 or 7 o'clock in the evening it is almost impossible to
get a table at Delmonico's, the Brunswick, and some of the
others; but, with the exception of a few unmarried men, there
are no regular habitués. It is the greatest mistake in the world
to suppose, as so many English do, that the mass of Americans

have no regular *home,* but live in hotels and boarding houses; and this even after English travellers have been in America and seen with their own eyes the vast number of charming private houses. They wonder at the extraordinary rapid growth of the towns, the rapid growth being the numberless "homes" which are springing up, and then because in their hotels they see a few "permanent boarders," they take it for granted that "the mass of Americans live in hotels." There are no people who travel as much as the Americans and, consequently, the hotels are always full, and a great many are too poor to possess a house. People marry on nothing, and the boarding-house is only looked upon as a temporary refuge, until the sole object of the man's work is gained, the possession of a "home."

In New York and all the great towns the private houses are wonderfully pretty and comfortable, so bright, fresh and gay-looking and full of every sort of comfort. The last "improvement" which every nice new private house thinks it must now have is a private telegraphic apparatus—in some houses it is only a signal telegraph. For instance: you want a message sent; you touch a certain signal and one of the corps of messengers appears. You hear a burglar in the house; you make the proper signal and immediately the police arrive; another signal and the fire brigade is aroused. We tried it at the house of a friend and touched the signal for a messenger; in exactly four minutes and a-half a little boy rang the hall-door bell to know what we wanted. But, if you wish really to be a swell, you have a regular telegraphic apparatus, a charming simple little instrument which you play upon, something like a piano,

and can have a nice little chat with your friends all over the
town without the slightest trouble, making society very easy.
I wonder when it will come in in London. What a conveni-
ence it would be in the season, but people are so frightfully
conservative in England and it is such ages before a novelty
can make its way. When we were here before, three years ago,
John[2] was so struck with the telegraphic apparatus which he
saw in all the great bankers' and merchants' offices. By the
side of the table was a little self-acting machine from which
poured a long narrow ribbon of white paper, on which was
stamped the news of the world as it came in to the Central
Telegraphic Office; a basket received the long rolls of paper.
They say it has only just been introduced into the business-
houses of London.

We drove in the Central Park this evening; it is growing
so wonderfully pretty as the trees are getting up. It was full
of fast-trotting teams, the horses in their very slight harness
and no blinkers look quite naked after those one is accus-

[2] My husband.

tomed to see in England, and when not trotting at full speed
they go along in a slouching sort of way, poking their heads
out, which is very ugly. We dined at Judge Parsons', who
showed us some wonderful Mexican knives.

Lennox, Mass.

September 12th—Yesterday afternoon I came here, Lennox,
Mass., in the Berkshire Hills, a charming resort of a very nice
set of people from New York, Boston and Philadelphia. The
air is deliciously pure and bracing and the drives in every direction are beautiful. There is a very nice new Club house for
gentlemen, and a large public room with a polished-oak floor
for dancing, and a stage at one end of it for theatricals, con-
certs, etc.

September 13th—To-day I drove with Ned Rogers through
Mr. Wolsey's place near here. He has an enclosed park of
2,000 or 3,000 acres, with about 10 miles of grass drives and
rides through rocky glens and over wooded hills with, occasionally, the most beautiful distant views over the far ranges.
The house is small and has no garden round it. Very few of
the American country places have the bright flower beds about
the house that one is accustomed to see in England. The summers are almost too hot and dry for "bedding-out" to succeed
well. At Newport and on the North River there are a few
places which look bright enough, but it is a pity it is not more
general, for they look so dull without it. But then, country life

altogether is so different here, in fact, there is no country life
for the upper classes. Many of them have villas and one or
two have large places like this of Mr. Wolsey's, but they come
to them for only a few months in the summer and generally
lead a very dull life. They have nothing to do, no estates to
look after, no shooting or sport of any kind whatever and very
little Society. During the heat of the day in summer one cannot stir out of doors, and a drive on the dusty roads in the
evening is all one has to look forward to. The autumn is the
pleasantest time, but even then there is absolutely nothing for
a man to do, and I do not wonder the whole family is delighted to get back to town early in October. Winter in the country
is intolerable for, generally, the roads are so bad that driving
is out of the question, excepting when there is sleighing for
a few weeks, which is certainly very enjoyable while it lasts,
but it is very uncertain, and when the frost goes the roads are
worse than ever. English people have often asked me if there
was no country life in America. There is none, and I am quite
sure that there never can be country life in America (I mean
for the rich upper classes) as it is understood in Europe. There
can never be any sport. Hunting would be impossible in any
of the Eastern or middle States: the fences are too enormously
high for any horse to jump, and the enclosures are all small,
besides the long-continued hard frosts, and the farmers never
would stand having their lands ridden over. There could be
no shooting, for game has almost entirely disappeared from
these States, excepting in some of the mountain districts,
where a few quail and partridge are found in the woods in the
autumn; and the owners of these lands cannot keep poachers

out of them, although there is a law of trespass. Sport and looking-after his estate are the only things that keep the rich Englishman, the German or Frenchman in the country for many months. In America there are only one or two large estates divided into farms and let to tenants, indeed, I only know of two; these are always cited as exceptional instances. One belongs to the Van Rennseler family, who have had an immense deal of trouble in making their tenants pay the rent; the other large estate is that belonging to my own people in the Geneseo Valley, but, from there being no law of primogeniture in America, it is being rapidly sub-divided into small portions, the owners of which sell whenever they can, generally to the occupying tenants, to reinvest their money at higher interest.

Americans, with their active energetic minds, could never settle down to do nothing in the country, and as they make their enormous fortunes, not having the outlet for them that a great estate and country place give, they look naturally to Europe, and find the amusements and brilliant life of Paris irresistible. Besides, is it not "the place where good Americans go when they die?" I am sure my own country people will agree with me when I say that Society in New York, or any of the large towns, is very unsatisfactory. The men are all absorbed in business and, during the day, are never seen "up town." There are no men of leisure; consequently, when a man of fortune in New York is not in business, there is nothing for him to do, and he has no companions to do nothing with, and so he goes to Europe and wastes his life in Paris. All New York is divided into small sets and the most exclusive

Society in the world is the "upper ten." There being no out-ward distinctions of class or rank, an imaginary barrier is formed of who is in Society and who is not, and it is utterly im-possible for any *nouveau riche* to penetrate it. I have heard of several families of *parvenus* who, finding this, have gone to Europe and established themselves in Paris and Rome in mag-nificent apartments and, entertaining splendidly, have been able to get into the very best Society and marry their daughters into great French and Roman families. They have then re-turned to New York to find the barrier as immovable as ever, their invitations unanswered and their rooms empty. Political distinction, I am sorry to say, is rather a barrier to good So-ciety all over the Union. To be a politician means so univer-sally to be something low that, when gentlemen are persuaded to hold some political place, their friends give them the great-est credit for sacrificing position and enduring such odium for the sake of their country. I am afraid this is principally owing to that horrid Irish vote, which seems to demoralize politics wherever it has anything to say to it.

New York Again

September 14th—I returned to-day to New York and went to our friend Mr. Hewitt's house, or rather to his father-in-law's —Mr. Peter Cooper, the most delightful of old gentlemen, who only lives to do good and be of use to his fellow-creatures. His vast fortune, made wholly by himself, is almost entirely devoted to benevolent enterprises. "The Cooper Institute," an enrmous building erected at his own expense and endowed by him with a large income, gives a gratuitous scientific education to any working-man who may choose to avail himself of it. Every evening 2,000 or 3,000 working-men are assembled in the schools, mechanics generally, mastering the technical difficulties of their trades. When Mr. Cooper was a struggling young man, clever and eager to advance himself, he found the great difficulty he had to fight against was the want of scientific knowledge; and there being no place where he could acquire such knowledge, without going to an expense that was impossible to him, and giving up his days which was also impossible, the first use he made of the large fortune which his untiring energy and cleverness placed at his disposal, was to help others struggling with the same difficulties which so often baffled himself. The Cooper Institute now affords facilities to thousands of clever young men who wish to gain information in their professions and raise themselves by education. It has also schools of design, etc.

Mr. Cooper, though now eighty-four years of age, takes as active an interest as ever in all these works, and indeed, in the opinion of all, there is no end to the good he does. His mind is as clear as a man of forty, and every new discovery in Science or Mechanics is discussed by him with as perfect an understanding and with as eager an interest as if he were only just starting in life.

September 15th—The heat yesterday and to-day has been so oppressive that it has made me quite ill. The delicious cool

Irish summers spoil one, and it is provoking to be caught by the heat when we had timed our visit especially to avoid it. In the afternoon we went over the Butler-Duncans' villa on Staten Island. It stands beautifully on an eminence overlooking New York bay, and it was so charming, watching the shipping passing to and fro, from the stateliest European steamer to the tiniest yacht. Just at the foot of the hill Lord Charleville's yacht is anchored, but he, poor fellow, is so ill that he is not able to leave it. He has been delicate for a long time and it was thought yachting would be good for him, but, while fishing in the Banks off Newfoundland, he caught fresh cold in those dank fogs and is now, they say, in a very precarious state.

September 17th—Yesterday we returned to New York from Mr. Duncan's and made our preparations to leave for the West. I am limited to the smallest possible amount of luggage, such a nuisance. I do like plenty of room for my things and luggage is so little trouble here too.

Journey to Lake Superior

We started on our journey to Lake Superior in the evening, and such an evening; the rain coming down in floods! Our party numbers fourteen. We have two cars entirely to ourselves. One is a Directors' car with a kitchen, dining-room, drawing-room filled with the most luxurious easy chairs, and a verandah at the back where the gentlemen sit and smoke, and

where, in a comfortable corner seat, I can see the country we are
being whirled through. The other car is a Pullman's sleeping
car, where they have given me a drawing-room compartment
with a little dressing-room attached—the perfection of comfort. At night the negro in charge of the car converts the seats
of the "drawing-room compartment" into the most civilized beds and sheets, blankets and pillows, and these enormous cars are so well made, the springs and counter-springs so
numerous, that one hardly feels any motion as they glide almost noiselessly along. The chief of our Party, Mr. Barnum, is
one of the principal "Iron men" in the States, and manages
any number of Iron mines and furnaces, both in New York,
Connecticut and Michigan—a man immensely respected and
looked up to, so upright, that, as the Bernal Osborne of our
party (for we *have* a B.O.) declares, "He is so upright, Sir,
that he leans over the other way." For the last three years he
has had the management of some Iron mines, near Marquette,
in which we are shareholders and, being anxious to show the
shareholders what he has done in the way of developing the
enterprise, he has made up this party, all people interested in
it: and the Railway Companies have placed these cars at his
disposal. I am the only lady and I never knew anything like
the kindness of everybody. Two of our party I found to be old
friends of my father, and as full of affection for him and of
admiration for his noble character as was everyone who knew
him.

Soon after leaving New York last night our train was
stopped in the middle of a forest; a freight train had broken
down in front of us, and for four hours we were kept waiting,

the rain coming down in a tropical down-pour, beating against our wooden box and coming in at the ventilators; sometimes it broke against us like a wave, and the great heavy car positively quivered and swayed under it like a ship: it almost seemed as if we should be washed away. To-day we have been crossing the Alleghany mountains; two large engines pulled us up the the steep inclines at the rate of forty miles an hour; the finest scenery, they say, we passed before dawn, but these densely-wooded mountains have exquisite spots in them, and I am never tired of looking out for them from my corner in the verandah, while I listen to the conversation going on amongst the gentlemen who are smoking, principally about stocks and mines, and I shall be able to give the most valuable advice to my friends in England upon all sorts of American invest-ments. The wonderful stories I hear them telling each other of how new Railways are floated are enough to make one's hair stand on end. As illustrating the wonderful resources of America, I am told of a young Scotchman who came to the States with only 2/6 in his pocket; at the end of ten years he *owed* 1,200,000 dollars!! What a country!

The train has been trying all day to make up the lost time, and the cook chose to give us dinner just as we had crossed the summit of the mountains and were tearing down the incline on the other side at the rate of sixty miles an hour, and it was almost impossible to keep anything on the table as we went swaying and jerking round the curves. However, it was a new sensation!

I had a long talk with Mr. Ogden to-day. He was one of the original founders of Chicago and owned an immense deal of property there. The great fire destroyed three or four millions of dollars' worth of his property. Like all clever far-seeing Americans he is alarmed at the degradation universal suffrage is bringing on politics in this country.

Chicago

September 18th—Arrived this evening at Chicago. The gorgeousness of the Palmer House Hotel quite took one's breath away. The usual negro boy shewed us up the white marble staircase, through the broad corridors decorated with a dado of white marble and innumerable mirrors, into the Egyptian "parlour," where we were amused, while waiting for our rooms, at seeing what an upholsterer gone mad could do. Sphinxes gazed at us from every direction, and a row of them, varied by a bull or two as a cornice over the windows, which were hung with bright green and red satin curtains, was very imposing. On each side great folding-doors led into other drawing-rooms ever more gorgeous. The carpets were beautiful, but Western men had an odious habit of spitting on them, though there were gorgeous spittoons or "cuspidors" about. I was told a story of a Western man who, visiting at the White House, spat continually upon the carpet. The negro servant placed one of these splendid spittoons in one direction: the Westerner turned the other way and spat on the other side of the chair: the darkie moved the spittoon and placed it there. "I

tell you, darkie," the man said, "if you don't take that orna-
ment out of the way, I'll spit right into it."

A wide corridor extended all round the hotel, and nearly all
day it was filled with numbers of people "promenading." Off
it opened the "Bridal Chambers," a series of most magnifi-
cently-decorated bedrooms. The carved wood furniture was
inlaid with ormolu and plaques of china. The curtains and covering of the chairs and sofas were the most brilliant-hued
satins and damasks, and an immense gaselier with about a
dozen burners hung from the ceiling. All these rooms seemed
empty and the doors were open for us to gaze and wonder. In
the evening, after dinner, we went to the State "Fair," an immense building brilliantly lighted and thronged with people
of all classes, where all the latest inventions were exhibited;
such wonderful reaping and mowing machines! There was
one "combination" machine to be drawn by two horses, one
man to drive and another standing on a sort of platform to
perform the work. It first cut the wheat, and then gathered it
in, threshed it and filled a sack with the grain; the sacks are
thrown on the ground to remain there in the dry climate for
days perhaps, until the farmer is ready to come with his team
and gather up the row of sacks, which is all that remains of
his enormous wheat-field, for the straw is of no use on these
enormous farms, where manure is little used, and is left on
the spot. There was a very good collection of modern pictures
exhibited at the "Fair," and one large picture representing a
buffalo bull in the act of charging, with his great head low-
ered, his red nostrils and glowing ferocious eyes, was very

striking; I was told that was what I should encounter on the
prairie. I was longing to buy it and send it home to Rathdaire.

September 19th—There was a delightful paragraph de-
scribing our party in the papers this morning:

"Great capitalists from the Eastern States who had arrived
at the Palmer House. Each of these gentlemen is able to clear
his cheque for a million!" which seemed a most charming
idea, and I wanted John to draw his cheque at once, but he
seemed to think there were objections!

Early this morning I sent letters of introduction to General
Sheridan, who very kindly called upon us at 11 o'clock. I had
never met him before, though my brother Craig was so long
on his staff and, of course, he knew my father. He was always
looked upon as the most gallant officer in the army, and his
troops were devoted to him. Nothing could exceed his kindness to us. He advised us to go to Sydney Barracks on the
Union Pacific Railway, to organise an expedition there, and go
to the Republican Valley, where there were always buffalo, besides other game, antelope, wild turkeys, etc. "Oh," I said, "I
am so glad we shall see wild turkeys, I want particularly to see
wild turkeys." The General's eyes twinkled, "You may come
across a famous place where I and my staff camped one night,
and we were just getting quiet for the night when from all
directions large flocks of wild turkeys came pouring in and
perched in the trees almost above our heads. We got out our
guns and in an hour or two we had killed 63 turkeys, and they
christened the place 'Sheridan's Roost'." He described the
state of the Indian warfare further South as making it quite

impossible for us to attempt a buffalo hunt lower down than the Republican. He told us that we must take a cavalry escort with us, and when we rather demurred as to the necessity and said, "Oh, surely we shall not want that," he replied, "You may not want them, but if you do want them, you'll want them like hell!!" So I suppose we had better have them! He also most kindly proposed to give leave to Colonel Dodge, who is a very mighty hunter, to accompany us. This will be a great help to us, for there are so few sportsmen in the United States, that it is almost impossible to get information of what is wanted on such an expedition as we propose making, or how to manage it. Colonel Dodge has a great reputation for organising the most successful hunting-parties, when enormous bags have been made. He is now stationed at Omaha, which is too far from the wild regions for him to get up expeditions of his own. General Sheridan says, of course I must go with them and that I shall enjoy it immensely.

Church time passed while we were wickedly settling all these matters, but we went out for a walk to see this wonderful city, which justly astonishes every stranger who sees it for the first time. We did not go to see a grain elevator! It seemed very odd to see all the shop-windows open and the goods arranged just as they would be on a week day, but the doors were shut. It seems that this is the custom here as a protection against burglars; no shutters are put up at night, the gas is left burning in the shop so that the policemen can see that all is right as they walk on their beats. Sometimes it does not quite answer however, for we heard that a few days ago a policeman passing a jewellery "store" saw the door open and a man standing near the doorway with a nonchalant air; he accosted the policeman in a very frank cheerful way, making some excuse for being obliged to come down to his store at that time of night, but his wife was ill and he had forgotten a bottle of medicine he had bought for her that day. I am afraid the policeman was made for better things, and more virtuous places than Chicago, for he passed on, and, alas, the next day the shop was found by its real proprietor denuded of everything valuable.

In the afternoon General Sheridan came for me and took me a most charming drive on the Boulevards, which is the name given to a broad beautifully-kept road, along the edge of the lake, bordered with gardens running for several miles, out to a new Park which promises to be very pretty. I had so much that was interesting to talk over with General Sheridan, Craig having been one of his aide-de-camps during all the time of his celebrated campaign in the Shenandoah Valley, when every day was filled with exciting incidents. Provisions sometimes were very short, and on one occasion Craig went out with a foraging party, their object being a mill lying on the edge of the enemy's country, where it was supposed a large quantity of flour was stored away. They arrived safely at the mill, dismounted and, leaving their horses in charge of a few troopers, most of the party entered the building to search for the coveted flour. Craig had mounted to the top storey of the immensely high building, and was in a large room without any windows but with one opening on the back of the mill, where there was a windlass for hoisting up flour and a rope attached to it. Suddenly he heard shouts and cries in the rooms beneath him, and discovered in an instant that the rebels had surprised them; he rushed to the opening and looking down he saw four or five of the rebels' horses held carelessly by one trooper. Quick as thought he seized the rope, slid down it to the ground, and before the rebel trooper had time to give the alarm he was on the back of one of the horses and galloping away. The rebels had come up at the back of the mill, where there were no windows and only one opening in the top storey for hoisting flour up by the windlass. They had left some of their horses and stolen around to the front, where they made a dash and succeeded in capturing the whole party except my brother. When he arrived in his own camp and dismounted, it occurred to him to look into the saddle-bags hanging to the saddle of the rebel's horse he had escaped upon, and in them he found a number of letters intended for General Sheridan's troops, evidently the contents of some mail-bag which had been captured by the rebels on its way, and amongst the letters my brother found one for himself from me! I had sent him my photograph but, of course, the letters had all been opened and it was gone.

When I returned from our drive I found John as full of astonishment and admiration of this wonderful town as I was; he had walked all over it, but he was amused at the sensation his light brown suit of check clothes had made; one group that he stood near declared he must be one of P. T. Barnum's men. Another man informed his friend that "That there is the uniform at Sing-Sing" (the great State prison) "I guess"; but this resemblance had been already pointed out in New York, where Mr. Hewitt's clerk entreated Mr. H. not to walk up

Broadway with John, as he was dressed exactly like the con-
victs at Sing-Sing. What would Mr. Poole say if he knew of
the indignities that are being heaped upon his nice brown and
white check, which I chose myself. In the evening we all dined
together and, after dinner, started for Lake Superior in the
same cars we had travelled in all the way from New York.

Peshtigo

September 20th—We travelled all night and this morning arrived at Peshtigo, the scene of the most terrible and heart-
rending incidents of the great fire which swept over the forest
in parts of the State of Michigan, at the very same time as the
Chicago fire was devastating that wonderful city. Peshtigo is a
small town on the banks of a river and entirely surrounded by
forest; indeed, the whole State of Michigan is one vast forest
with a few settlements and towns on the edge of Lakes Michigan and Superior. The autumn of 1871 was very dry and fires
broke out at various places in the forest. Mr. Ogden owns all
the land about Peshtigo and large tracts of forest; he has immense saw-mills and a great number of men employed cutting
timber. On the day after he heard that three millions of his
property had been swept away by fire in Chicago, and he was
on his way from New York to investigate his losses, he received a telegram telling him that fires were raging at different
points in his tract of forest land in Michigan, that the flames
had swept over the town of Peshtigo, entirely destroying every

house, and that 160 people had lost their lives. It was too true! As the train stands still on the bridge, and I look out on that placid river winding through the flourishing-looking town which has sprung up again, I can hardly realise the scenes of horror that were enacted there so short a time before. For weeks before that fatal day the air had been clouded with smoke and there were vague rumours of forest fires at distant points, as usual at the end of the dry American summers.

The morning of the 10th October dawned brilliant and bright, as only an American October morning can, the trees were gaudy in their autumnal tints, and the sun shone dazzlingly, but a furious wind roared through the tall fir-trees in the forest. About midday some men at work in the open air felt suddenly a hot blast on their faces; they looked around them; in the brilliant sunlight at first no flames could be seen, but the roar in the forest was greater than that of the wind alone. The fire—the fire was upon them! As suddenly as this, without a moment's warning the flames, borne swiftly before the wind, swept over the quiet peaceful village and sheets of fire enveloped every house, all built of wood. No pen can describe the wild agony and despair and confusion of that moment; all rushed from their houses; many tried to run before the flames, those all perished; others rushed to the river and these were the only ones that were saved, but of these only the strong. All that day and night they stood up to their necks in the water, many holding little children in their arms, and, continually dashing the water over their heads, they managed to preserve life, in spite of the fire blazing all about them as long as there was anything left to burn. In the morning the flames abated, and the survivors, weak and exhausted, all more or less suffering from burns, dragged themselves up the river banks to gaze upon the scene of blackened destruction before them, their homes all gone, their families broken up. It was too horrible! Three years have passed and the town of wooden houses is again standing in the middle of its clearing, and the forest is there, only a little further off, but not green and living; the great blackened trunks still stand upright, their branches gone, just as the fire left them, too impatient to sweep on towards fresh food to consume entirely those stout masses. Years will pass before they will decay and cease to remind the dwellers in Peshtigo of that horrible day and night.

Lake Michigan

We left our train here for a couple of hours, and, by a small branch line belonging to Mr. Ogden, we went down to the port on Lake Michigan where he has a huge saw-mill: we went all over it and inspected every process, from the huge log being caught by grapnels in the canal and hauled up to the mill and under the machinery, as easily as if it was a cigar; first the two rough sides were shaved off, then it was shoved through a row of saws which cut it up instantly into six or eight boards which, after a little pushing and shoving about, came out in bundles of laths, all in less than a quarter-of-an-hour. A great deal of this wonderful machinery has been invented by Mr. Ogden, and it was delightful to see how he en-

joyed watching the beautiful way it worked. I confess I
thought there was too much roar and whizzing and banging
and great logs walking about apparently without any human
aid, and beams popping out just where one was going to step,
and streams of sawdust suddenly pouring down a shoot at
one's shoulders.

At 12 o'clock we were *en route* again, passing through interminable forests. All day long our line ran monotonously
along a perfectly flat country; occasionally, the train stopped
at a little cluster of log houses, occupied generally by Swedes
or Norwegians, who had cleared a little garden, and were
burning charcoal for the iron furnaces further North. There
was never a real break in the view, but always trees, trees,
trees, sometimes tall strong pines, then long stretches of
wretched hemlocks, sometimes beech and maple, and often
for miles blackened trunks alone, where the breath of the fire
demon had scorched and withered. I was so glad when we
reached Negaunee, with all its iron mines and furnaces.

Negaunee

Our party divided here; some remained and slept at the
Boarding House which is kept for the employees of the Iron
Cliff Mines, and some of us came to Marquette, a charmingly-
situated town on the banks of Lake Superior, where we found,
as usual, a very good hotel with "supper" going on, but I was
so intent on making out the extraordinary coiffures of the

waitresses, that the charms of white fish and teal and raw tomatoes and Catawba grapes were quite thrown away upon me.
These gorgeous young ladies live in the town; they perform
none of the menial work of the dining-room, but, after the
table is laid and everything arranged by a slave in the hotel,
for a "consideration" they come in and allow themselves to be
admired, while they wait upon you, with a languid grace
which would not have been so ridiculous if they had only been
in the least good-looking. Mr. Blackmore went out to buy
some photographs and came in after we had finished our meal.
The young ladies had gone to their homes, and the hotel-
keeper told him he could not give him anything to eat that
night, but he might be able to get something at the "restaurant" down-street, which, accordingly, he was obliged to do,
or starve.

September 21st—After an early walk on the heights over the
Lake we returned to Negaunee and joined the rest of the
party. Three or four carriages were provided for us and we
drove to see one iron mine and furnace after another all day
long, until my brain quite reeled with looking down into deep
excavations and up extraordinary chimneys, not to speak of all
the information that was given me about hematite ore and
magnetic ore, etc. I tried to understand, but found the only
thing that really made an impression was the ore with jasper in
it; the jasper was beautiful but, as it could not be separated
from the iron and the iron could not be got away from the jasper, they were both useless, and great heaps of it, which had
been put out before good ore could be reached, were lying

about waiting for somebody to invent a process for separating them. The shareholders seemed very much pleased with the richness of the mines and general prosperity. Even the fearful roughness of the roads did not interfere with the good humour of the capitalists; but then a road can afford to be very rough, even for six long miles, when it leads to an iron mine which is making a profit of 10 per cent in bad times. I suggested 5 per cent for one year and a good road, but they did not "see it." The whole region is iron, and new mines are being discovered every day. Everybody one met, in fact, had a mine to sell and the price was always 100,000 dollars!

As soon as John and Mr. Blackmore were discovered to be Englishmen they were constantly surrounded by various seedy-looking individuals, who possessed most valuable mines which, "as times were hard, they were willing to dispose of on reasonable terms"—only 100,000 dollars! There was one shopkeeper in Negaunee who had a mine he pressed on them very strongly. He had only become possessed of it a short time before in the following way. His shop is connected with one of the great iron companies and much trusted by everyone in the neighbourhood. He had only recently taken the manage-ment of it. One day two "prospectors" came in in great spirits; they had been in the forest for weeks searching for traces of iron ore on Government land, and had at last discovered indi-cations of what they considered a very valuable mine, and were on their way to the Land Office at Marquette that eve-ning to record their claim for the land. The shopkeeper gave this account of the affair with great triumph to one of our party: "Well, Sir," he said, "I just wormed out of them in a casual way, while I sold 'em a bottle of pickles, the exact situation of that discovery of theirs, and, the minute they left the shop, up I sloped to the telegraph office, and before they had got to the Depot to start for Marquette, I wired a friend of mine in that city to record my claim for that bit of land. Yes, Sirree, I did, and I'll sell it to you now for 100,000 dollars." But he did not describe the feelings of those two poor fellows who, after enduring weeks of hardship and toiling with hammer and spade, had at last discovered what they thought was to make their fortune, and with buoyant hearts entered the Land Office, to find that only an hour before some wretch had stolen away from them the fruits of their labour.

Michiganni City

September 22nd—We slept last night at Negaunee and this morning came by train to the Michiganni Iron Mines, but I was not well and, as one iron mine is not unlike another, I took it for granted that this one is to yield 50, nay, 100 per cent profit in a year or two, and did not insist upon seeing with my own eyes, so I remained in the car (our old friend from New York) enjoying the view over the beautiful wild lake, with its hilly shores and islands covered with woods, every leaf coming out so distinctly in this clear Northern air, which to breathe is like taking a glass of champagne, and at one end the cluster of small new wooden houses and saw-mills forming "Michiganni City," where only three years ago the Indians' wigwam was to be seen, and yet Michiganni City has been once in its short life entirely destroyed by fire and is only just rebuilt. I was told a "most delightful little New England lady" lived in one of those new brown wooden houses, and so I went to see her, and found such a charming pretty young bride—Mrs. Fowle—in the freshest, brightest little drawing-room, and over the door was written in letters of flowers: *"God bless our Home."* Her husband was an employee of the Company and had brought his young wife from far-off Massachusetts. She said she liked the summer very much, the air was perfect, though the black flies were rather disagreeable and the "mosquitoes as big as birds," but she was afraid the winter would be very bad; they had told her *such* stories of the frightful cold. She had a delightful Pomeranian dog— "Crow," a most independent-looking person, whose head was rather turned by just having a street called after him and, consequently, seemed to think the whole town belonged to him. Our big car got off the rails and everybody was obliged to assist in lifting it back with crowbars, etc. This was a proceeding which "Crow" (he was perfectly white) did not understand at all, and which he evidently thought was not to be tolerated for an instant in his domain. He ran up and down in the most furious state of excitement and, if he saw anyone working particularly hard, he fastened himself on to the leg of his trousers, and pulled back with all his might, which several of our capitalists thought very unpleasant. In the evening we returned to Negaunee and, bidding all our kind friends good-bye, we came on to Marquette to take the steamer on Lake Superior for Duluth.

September 23rd—We found the steamer *Metropolis* lying at her wharf, the bell ringing furiously as if she was off instantly. We seemed to be almost the only passengers, the long gorgeously-furnished saloon had no one in it, but although the evening was warm there was a great stove at each end nearly red-hot. Everyone on board was most uncivil. I never saw such a set of people, and I don't wonder at the paucity of passengers, although the bell went on ringing for an hour before she at last started.

Lake Superior

The moon shone brightly over the heights above the town and, with all the lights on the margin of the water, it was a lovely scene as we steamed away into the great Lake. The steward was lounging about smoking a cigar, and would not deign to notice us or show us our cabins until it suited his august pleasure. Although we were to be two days and two nights on board, the people who had charge of the luggage positively refused to allow us to have any in our cabins, as it was "not allowed." We could only take our handbags, but this was too much to stand and, before they knew what he was going to do, John took up our two small portmanteaux, one in each hand, rushed upstairs with them and deposited them in our cabins. Some of the men followed him talking very fiercely but, apparently, thought it best not to push matters any further. This was only the beginning of our troubles and we ought to have left the boat, but we were very anxious to get to Duluth with as little delay as possible, and it was very uncertain if another steamer would stop at Marquette for several days. We could get no food yesterday evening but a cup of half-cold tea and a bit of bread. Breakfast this morning was almost as bad. We stopped in the morning at several places, and John and Mr. Blackmore went ashore and visited the famous Copper mines.

At Portage the boat stopped so long that we enquired the reason, and were told that the Captain had a lawsuit going on in the Court there, and we should probably have to remain all day! It was quite true, the Captain and most of his crew have gone ashore, and we have been kept here the whole day! John went up to the Court to see what it was all about. It seems, a few weeks ago the steamer was loading wood, and about two cords of wood belonging to someone else was taken by mistake, and the trial turned on the quantity taken and the quality of the wood; the Captain said it was two cords; the other side declared it was four. After considerable searching John discovered that the trial was going on in an upper-room in a small corner-house, over a shop; to the door of the room was attached a neat card with "A. Dodge—Justice of the Peace," inscribed upon it. On entering he found in a sweltering atmosphere, amid innumerable flies, a nervous old gentleman sitting at a table, on one side of which were grouped the Captain, the Mate and his Attorney, and on the other, his adversary with a like Professional assistance; one or two witnesses completed the party. Some had their coats off and some were

engaged in the national occupation of whittling, all were expectorating. The evidence was not taken in a rapid manner,
and proceeded much as follows:

Attorney to Witness: "You saw the wood?"

Witness: "Wal, I guess I did."

Attorney: "Now, what kind of wood was it?"

Witness (after a pause): "Wal, there were several kinds."

Attorney: "How much of each kind?"

Witness: "Wal—I couldn't just calkilate."

Attorney: "What was the value of the wood?"

Witness: "Wal"—(pause, much expectoration)—"Wal,
wood has different values"—and so on.

As all these important answers were accompanied with much
expectoration and given with great hesitation, John "con-
cluded" to come away, and returned with most desponding
views of the termination of the suit. The heat has been excessive all day: the boat lying close under the hill is a regular sun-
trap; the dinner uneatable and I have been anything but
flourishing.

September 24th—Still on the steamer. We ought to have arrived this morning. Very miserable all day. The shores very
uninteresting: no break in the interminable forest coming
down to the water's edge.

September 25th—We arrived this evening at Duluth, and very
glad we were to leave the *Metropolis*, where we had passed
three most uncomfortable days: at least, I had. Yesterday was
another very hot day. We steamed slowly along with the shore

always in sight, always the same dark line—endless unbroken primeval forest stretching away inland as far as the eye could see, and for many hundred miles beyond. Two or three times we stopped at little settlements and passengers got in and out. At one place John got out to try and buy a little milk for me. He found some at an Irishwoman's, who insisted upon giving it to him when she heard it was for a lady who was ill. He asked her if she would not like to return to the old country. "Ah yes, Sir, I should indeed, but I shall always remain here; I could not leave my child." "Where is your child, Ma'am?" "There, Sir," pointing to the graveyard on the hillside, "she lies there and I shall never go away from her." We had a very nice Norwegian boy on board; he had travelled all the way from Trondjhem quite alone, and he could not speak a word of English. The rudeness and incivility of everybody connected with the boat, from the Captain down, increased every day. John bought a few eggs, as the food was quite uneatable; he asked the steward to have them cooked, and the answer was, "Wal, I guess you had better go down to the kitchen and cook 'em yourself"; which he did.

The passengers were very queer people; there was one old man of sixty with a young wife of fourteen with a baby almost as big as herself, and at one place where we stopped, we saw a boy and girl of about fourteen, who we were told were a married couple!

The sunsets were the most beautiful I ever saw or imagined. As we turned towards the open sea the horizon and all the heavens filled with masses of the most brilliant-hued clouds, heaped up into mountains of crimson and gold and purple,

and weird castles and fairy-like distant cities, changing in colour every moment, and all reflected in the perfectly-smooth
lake as we moved over it; while, on the other side was the great
contrast of the dark, still unchanging, mournful line of forest
coming down to the water's edge—so still and so mysterious,
as night came on and gloom settled over it. A few Indians still
wander about under the tall pines and grim hemlocks, making
their wigwams by the side of the running streams and living
on the trout in the pools and the deer which come down to
drink. A few wild men rough it in those gloomy solitudes,
prospecting for mines near the shores of the Lake, where beds
of copper and iron are supposed to be plentiful. As we approached the end of the Lake where Duluth lies we passed
through the Apostle Islands, all wooded—all exactly alike. It
was lucky the weather had been perfectly fine while we were
on the Lake, or we might have been detained even longer than
we were; we were thankful to have had such a smooth passage
for, sometimes, they have violent gales on the Lake and terrific waves. The great unwieldy steamers always make for the
nearest port at the slightest sign of a storm. They would not
be in the least fit to cope with a gale, and they do not pretend
to be.

Duluth

This town of Duluth is the terminus of the Northern Pacific
Railway and, during the time Jay Cooke was pushing that

"concern," and before the great "panic" of 1873, it was supposed to be a wonderfully-rising place, and the country all
around was laid out in "town lots" in which everyone was
speculating in the most frantic manner and, I believe, it was
not unknown even to London capitalists. There was a famous
speech made about it in Congress at the time the Northern Pacific Railway Land Grant was being "put through," and I
have jotted down some extracts which were given me which
show the flights American eloquence can take sometimes:

If gentlemen will examine the map they will find the town of
Duluth exists in the centre of a series of concentric circles, one
hundred miles apart and some of them as much as four thousand
miles in diameter, embracing alike in their tremendous sweep the
fragrant savannas of the Sunlit South and the eternal solitudes of
snow that mantle the ice-bound North. The fact is, Sir, Duluth is
pre-eminently a Central place . . . and I see it is represented on this
map as situated exactly half-way between the latitudes of Paris and
Venice, so that gentlemen who have inhaled the exhilarating airs of
the one or basked in the golden sunlight of the other, may see at
a glance that Duluth must be a place of untold delights—a terrestial
Paradise, fanned by the balmy zephyrs of an eternal spring, clothed
in the gorgeous sheen of ever-blooming flowers, and vocal with the
silver melodies of nature's choicest songsters. As to the commercial resources of Duluth, they are simply illimitable and inexhaustible, as is shown by this map. I see it stated here that there is a vast
scope of territory embracing an area of over 3,000,000 square miles,
rich in every element of material wealth and commercial prosperity, all tributary to Duluth. Look at it, Sir. Here are inexhaustible
mines of gold, immeasurable veins of silver, impenetrable depths of
boundless forest, great coal measures, enormous wheat-fields—all
embraced in this vast territory, only waiting for this Railway to be
made to pour their untold treasures into the the lap of Duluth and,

Sir, I am satisfied that Duluth is destined to be the great beef-market of the world. Here, you will observe (pointing to the map) are the Piegan Indians and here are the buffalo, and here are the Creeks. Now, Sir, when the buffaloes are sufficiently fat from grazing on these immense wheat-fields, you see, it will be the easiest thing in the world for the Piegans to drive them down, stay all night with their friends the Creeks and go into Duluth in the morning. I think I see them now, Sir—a vast herd of buffaloes with their heads down, their eyes glaring, their tongues out, and their tails curled over their backs, tearing along towards Duluth with a thousand Piegans on their ponies yelling at their heels, and as they sweep past the Creeks they join in the chase, and away they all go, yelling, bellowing, tearing along amid clouds of dust, until the last buffalo is safely penned in the stockyards at Duluth. Sir, I might stand here for hours and expatiate with rapture on the gorgeous prospects of Duluth, but human life is too short and the time of the House too valuable to allow me to linger longer upon the delightful theme.

Poor Duluth! it is in such an utter state of collapse now, and looked most wretched. The Northern Pacific Railway is completely smashed, and that was the only thing that was ever to make its greatness, for, although it may be the same latitude as Venice and Paris, the winters are long and frightfully cold, and the whole of the neighbouring country is a vast unbroken forest.

September 26th—In a drizzling rain this morning Duluth looked more dispirited than ever, as the omnibus that conveyed us to the station laboured through the deep mud-holes. The valuable "corner lots," squared and fenced, but still covered with the primeval forest or the primeval stumps, seemed most uninviting investments, and the swamp spread out below

the town suggested malaria and mosquitoes. Superior City, on
the other side of the bay, is a formidable rival and is a city of
great expectations, being, they say, better situated. The morning was close and muggy, but, when we got into the car, there
was the inevitable stove, red-hot, every window shut tight and
three babies! Pullman does not "run" his "drawing-room
coaches" on this line, and we were obliged to be content with
the ordinary car which holds about sixty people. There is a passage down the centre and the seats are arranged in twos on
each side. Soon after we left Duluth the day cleared up, and
the scenery we were passing through was so beautiful, that we
went out and stood on the "platform" at the back of the car,
much to the delight of the people inside, who were able then
to shut up all the windows we had opened and thoroughly
enjoy the close stove-heat and stuffy smells.

The St. Louis River

For miles we ran parallel with the St. Louis River, but several
hundred feet above it. Below us the broad river broke over its
rocky bed in mad torrents of foaming water, forming what are
called the Dalles of the St. Louis—a series of rocky waterfalls,
some of them most beautiful, with intervals of very steep rapids interspersed with wild picturesque-looking islands covered
with a tangled mass of trees and creepers: weird-looking hemlocks, hurled headlong by the storm over the raging stream,
cast wavering shadows in the foam. On the opposite side the

banks rose precipitately hundreds of feet above the water, sometimes too precipitately for any vegetation to grow, but generally with wooded sides: the woods were filled with maple and sumach, just beginning to get a scarlet tinge, which brought out the deep dark green of the fir and hemlock. Every few miles our train would "slow-off" until we hardly seemed moving at all and, almost breathless, it would creep gently on to one of those wonderful trestlework bridges which Railway Companies in America construct across the deepest and widest ravines. They seem a slight network of timber, like those spider-webs one sees in the early morning on the long grass, and on the top the immensely heavy train is poised on a single line of rails without any side protection whatever. It made me so dizzy looking down from such a great height that I could not stay outside, when we were on these bridges, and we had nine or ten to cross. At intervals, on a little projection, a barrel of water is placed in case of fire. Some of these bridges were made not straight but on a curve, and it was really frightful to see the train twisting over them, and going so slowly that one had plenty of time to think of everything that might happen, and how excessively unpleasant it might be. A friend of ours once asked the Engineer on one of these curved trestlework bridges on the Catawissa Line, which is as notorious as this line for its perilous bridges, if they were not thought dangerous. "Wal, it depends on how folks takes it," was his only reply.

The stations we were passing were only little clearings in the forest but, at mid-day, in one of these primitive-looking settlements surrounded by stumps, they gave us an excellent dinner, with trout, venison steaks and woodcock, tomatoes, pears and grapes, and they told us there were plenty of deer in the woods and the river was filled with trout and other fish. One of the photographs Mr. B. bought in Duluth represented a fisherman on the edge of a pool above some rapids with such a heap of fish of different kinds by his side, some very large. When we were standing on the platform a small boy of about eleven with a large gun on his shoulder, came out and began talking to us. He started the conversation by asking John if he was fond of "gunning." "Wal, I have splendid hunting in them woods—I go into 'em every few days and fetch out as many woodcocks as we can eat, and fine eating they are tew." We were just passing one of the most beautiful waterfalls— "That's fine water power, ain't it, Sir." In a few years the exquisite beauty of these Dalles will probably be entirely destroyed. The bed of the river is, they say, the finest slate-quarry in the United States, and already a Company is being formed to work the quarry with the water-power on the spot. But to most Americans their great beauty is their water-power. Even Niagara has many of its finest views destroyed by the obtrusive saw-mills and paper-factory. But the most comprehensive idea we have heard yet of utilizing Niagara was that of the American gentleman who proposed to turn the whole power of the Falls to work a huge waterwheel, the shaft of which should extend "right across our Union—then, Sir, anyone who wants power has nothing to do but belt on!"

St. Paul

In the afternoon we got into a beautiful open country covered with thick luxuriant-looking grass, and studded with nice groups of oak trees. Large herds of cattle were grazing over it, and the villages began to look more thriving as we approached St. Paul. We saw several parties of sportsmen with very good-looking dogs. St. Paul is considered the best place in America for prairie-chicken shooting, and we heard afterwards of two English friends of ours who went there in August of this year for a month's shooting, but they both said it was a mistake. They were very much disappointed.

At about six we arrived in St. Paul and for the first time we looked upon the Mississippi River—a grand river even here, though 1,500 miles from its mouth. The town of St. Paul is a rambling, straggling and, when we saw it, a very muddy place, with one good street, on a high bluff over the river. We found a capital hotel, where they gave us some delicious prairie-chicken for supper; and we were told they were shot by the hotel-keeper, who was now camping out on a sporting expedition up the country.

September 27th—Sunday. John and Mr. Blackmore went off early to visit the falls of St. Antony and Minnehaha. I enjoyed a day of quiet and rest. They came back late, very much disappointed. Minnehaha was a delusion and a snare, by no means equal to a Welsh or Scotch third-rate mountain-stream; and the falls of St. Antony, so celebrated, and the only falls on the Mississippi River, they found so divided and sub-divided

for flour and saw-mill purposes, that there was actually no
water left to go over the rocks which used to make falls in the
channel of the river. To-morrow we are to take the steamboat
down the Mississippi, which they say is very fine from here to
St. Louis.

Down the Mississippi

September 28th—We were to leave early this morning but the
steamboats are very irregular, and ours did not arrive till mid-
day, and then we were told it would not leave until evening, so
we resigned ourselves to seeing the lions of the town, only,
unfortunately, there were no lions to see. Every one of these
new Western towns is exactly like the others. There are generally a dozen large Churches, all very hideous, several immense brick school-houses, a few comfortable-looking detached villas belonging to "our most prominent citizens," a
row of irregular shops, or rather "stores," a gigantic hotel or
two and, scattered in and out amongst them all, a number of
small wooden houses and shanties and innumerable "saloons":
fill up the interstices with mud and dust, and the town is there.
The streets are not paved and are either covered with deep
mud-holes or heaps of dust. A plank sidewalk is made for
foot-passengers and is a very nice dry, clean, walk. St. Paul
was rather famous for its fur trade from the North, and I saw
some beautiful skins of silver fox, but the trade has dimin-
ished. Mr. Blackmore got some interesting Indian relics and a

beautiful piece of bead-work. The air here is deliciously pure and clear, and great numbers of consumptives come here from the Eastern States, even though the winters are so very severe. We have just heard that the steamboat will not leave until morning!

September 29th—At last the Captain made up his mind that he had secured all the freight to be got in St. Paul, and had tried the passengers' patience long enough, and at eleven this morning we went on board. A very black negro received us and took us up to the saloon, off which our cabins open. This saloon is about 200 feet long and 20 feet wide. At the lower end is a bar for the sale of cocktails, cigars, etc., and the upper end is very handsomely furnished, and is supposed to be the ladies' cabin. The day was warm and balmy but, as usual, two great stoves were in full blast in the saloon. Around the one nearest the bar a number of very rough-looking men were crowding, generally with high boots over their trousers, slouched hats, and all with belts and a mysterious-looking lump under their coats, at the side, where the Derringer is usually worn. All, who could, sat with their feet perched upon the top of the stove; the others loafed about with their hands in their pockets, waiting for their turn to come to enjoy this pleasure. None of them spoke, they were too busy chewing tobacco and expectorating in every direction. Near the other stove a lot of delicate-looking women were huddled, rocking themselves and chatting in highly-pitched whining voices, and over-run by a dozen children. The heat was so suffocating I could not bear it at all, but all day long the two stoves had their devoted groups. The families are principally Southern people who had been spending a part of their summer at the North, and are now returning to their homes in the Southern part of the Mississippi Valley; some of them have a very Creole look, and they all speak with the "Southern drawl" which is so irritating to ears not accustomed to it. There is one very smart lady in an elaborate brown toilette, her face covered with pearl-powder (an old Creole lady tells me it is not pearl-powder, but egg-shells pounded up very fine, and that "nothing is so good for the complexion"), and under her arm a small half-shaven poodle called "Dodo." Her husband wears a black evening coat and tall hat, of course; they are most lively amusing people, "in the hardware," as they tell us, and quite the life of the party. Outside the saloon there is a sort of verandah all the way round, but to-day this is covered with sheets, etc., hung to dry, all the washing of the steamer being done on board. We have discovered a charming place to sit— the roof of the saloon, quite in the bow; it is not generally used as a deck and there are only a low parapet around and a very slippery floor of pitch, where I see many tumbles. We stop very often to-day. There are no wharves, but the steamer simply bumps up against the shore. Though, apparently, so enormous, she draws only three feet of water, and the lower deck is like an immense platform projecting far out all the way round, and it is this platform that touches the shore; on it all the cargo is stowed, and above it is built up the great saloon with all the small cabins, etc. There is still a small third storey in the centre round the wheel-house, where the negro servants sleep.

Our first stoppage after leaving St. Paul was at some flour mills; a double line of wooden rails was hurriedly laid down from the mills to the steamboat, and then for two long hours a continuous stream of flour barrels, 1,000 they said, came rolling and bouncing down to the boat. All the loafers of the town assembled to watch the operation, lounging about, whittling sticks with their knives, and, of course, expectorating. A lot of pigs found it worth their while to attend in the ceremony, to feed on the flour which was shaken from the barrels.

The banks of the river to-day were very pretty, low wooded hills and large trees growing to the edge of the water. Our dinner was not very good, but the people are so civil and anxious to do anything for us. The waiters are all black, except the head waiter, who is a great swell. After tea the tables were all cleared away in the centre of the saloon, and a band of music made its appearance, the performers being some of the negro waiters. They played uncommonly well. First an overture from some opera, then one of them sang in an odd very high tenor voice—some most heart-breaking melodies—his whole body writhing in the most comical way during the affect-

ing parts, and his eyes rolling about to such a degree that only
the whites of them were visible in the middle of his jet-black
face. About nine they began playing a quadrille: the head-
waiter, who had been buzzing about in an important way,
came up to our end of the saloon—selected the prettiest of the
Creole-looking young ladies for a partner—the freight-agent
and others followed his example and the ball began. The long
saloon sloped down slightly in the centre where the dancing
was going on—and the *coup d'œil* from our upper end down
on the dancers and negro orchestra, and beyond to the bar
with its crowd of roughs (apparently taking an interest in the
ball) was very curious and amusing. There was one big negro
at the bass viol who called out all the figures—which were
very complicated and different from ours. Above the din of
the music and noises of the steamer, one heard him roaring
out at the top of his voice: "Ladies' chain—Gents to the right
—Dos à dos—Allemand all—Ladies in the centre—Prom-
en-ade," etc.; occasionally, a prolonged steam-whistle drowned
everything. The lady in brown was very much appreciated;
her unhappy poodle was generally given to some wall-
flower to hold, but the separation was intolerable to his
feelings, and, after whining and barking furiously for some
time, he always managed to burst from his holder's arms and
rush into the middle of the quadrille, where he was invariably
stepped upon, and set up a dreadful howl, before his lovely
mistress perceived him. Her husband was in his element. She
had already said to us—"he knows how to dance, he does," so
we watched his steps with interest, and they were certainly
most curious and wonderful. Near me was sitting a man who

had one wooden leg and was very much crippled, but the
music threw him into the greatest state of excitement; he beat
time with his crutches and nodded his head—his eyes gleam-
ing with delight. When the second quadrille was beginning,
he turned to me and said, "Guess I should be asking you to
figure round with me now, if I hadn't a-deposited that-air
leg on the fields of Gettysburgh. I used to be a great hand at
dancing, you bet!"[3] I rashly asked him how he had happened
to "deposit" his leg at Gettysburgh, and he immediately began
and gave me a full account of the battle and everything that
had happened to him in it—evidently an oft-told tale—and he
prolonged it over two quadrilles and a polka.

The ball went on until late. The Captain of the boat, a very
tall, gaunt man, occasionally joined in it, performing the most
elaborate steps with the greatest gravity—his head high in the
air—and always dancing with a short, fat, little woman, whom
he held at arm's length. The boat stopped longer than usual
at one place, and we left the saloon and went on deck, where
we were charmed by the exquisite beauty of the scene. We had
stopped at a small town lying at the foot of a hill. The landing-place and all the lower part of the boat were lighted up by
two braziers filled with flaming wood from the furnaces, on
which oil had been poured, making an uncertain, lurid light,
amid which the crew were moving quickly to and fro, like

[3] At first I never could understand this expression, which is much
used in the West—and also "You git"—until the two were explained
to me in the following anecdote: A burglar attacked a house, when the
owner, hearing a noise, went to the window, and, as the burglar was
stepping in, he placed the pistol to his head and called out, "You git";
to which the burglar only answered, "You bet," and made off.

creatures in the lower regions. It was a singular sight, wonderfully beautiful, but only lasted a few moments: we soon
cast off from the shore and the blazing fuel was carried back to
the fires. Near us a high, bold, projecting rock overhung the
water, and above, the moon had just risen—an exquisite young
moon, hardly out of its crescent, and seeming so pale and frag-
ile by the side of the brightened lights of the boat and the
town. The calm river spread out into a broad lake, shining like
a sea of silver; and, as I leant over the bows taking in all this
wondrous scene, as we floated gently down in the quiet moon-
light, the story of the rock above us was told to me.

Lake Pepin

We were in Lake Pepin, the most beautiful part of the Mississippi River, and which for our sins we were condemned to
pass through in the night-time. Its shores are embayed in
beautiful wooded hills and bold over-hanging rocks, with
here and there a yellow pebbly beach, where the rarest agates
and cornelians are still found.

The Lover's Leap

The rock before us, which rose seven or eight hundred feet
from the water's edge, was called "The Lover's Leap." It is
not so many years ago that the Indians yet roamed over the

Prairies that extend away for miles from the hills which border the river. A favourite camping-place of the Sioux were the shores of Lake Pepin, and the story runs that a beautiful Indian girl, the daughter of a great Sioux chief, in despair at being forced by her father into a marriage with a man she disliked, threw herself from the summit of this rock, in the presence of all the tribe, and sank into the water beneath, never to be seen alive again. It was so late that we could not stay up longer and, reluctantly, went to our little cabins for the night.

September 30th—Immediately after breakfast I went up to my place in the bow. Ah, how lovely the scene was! The wooded bluffs rose high in every varied form on one side of us, and the other was broken into innumerable islands covered thickly with large trees, through which the morning-sun glinted with the most beautiful soft light, giving an indescribably transparent, feathery, look to the foliage. The river was so calm and glassy that every branch and leaf was reflected; and over all a light silvery haze came and went, showing new mysterious-looking channels among the islands, then closing in until only the foreground was visible—but why attempt to describe it?— only poets should write of such scenes of enchantment. We floated dreamily down for hours without stopping, the bluffs sometimes becoming higher and bolder, growing into extraordinary shapes of ramparts and cornices; often we seemed really approaching an old feudal castle perched on the top of some bold crag, or a single column stood out like a monument over the river, then it would all change to a series of dome-like hills, the islands only varying in beauty; over some the wild grape-vine grew in great clinging masses, covering the trees entirely, like a gracefully-draped mantle, and falling over the banks until actually caught by and trailed in the current of the river. I could not but think of Longfellow's exquisite "Evangeline"; it was down this beautiful river that the band of Acadian exiles, "guided by hope and by hearsay sought for their kith and kin." With them Evangeline went in an endless search and endeavour to find Gabriel, the lover who had been torn from her so cruelly:

Day after day they glided adown the turbulent river;
Night after night by their blazing fires encamped on its borders.
Now through rushing chutes, among green islands where plume-
    like
Cotton trees nodded their shadowy crests, they swept with the
    current,
Then emerged into broad lagoons, where silvery sand bars
Lay in the stream, and, along the wimpling waves of their margin,
Shining with snow-white plumes, large-flocks of pelicans waded.

It was on one of these sylvan islands that the weary travellers slumbered when—

                              Nearer and ever nearer,
Darted a light, swift boat, that sped away over the water,
Urged in its course by the sinewy arms of hunters and trappers,
Northward its prow was turned to the land of the bison and beaver.
At the helm sat a youth with countenance thoughtful and careworn,
Dark and neglected locks overshadowed his brow, and a sadness
Somewhat beyond his years on his face was legibly written.
Gabriel was it who weary with waiting, unhappy and restless,
Sought in the Western wilds oblivion of self and of sorrow,

Swiftly they glided along, close under the lee of the island,
But by the opposite bank and behind a screen of palmettos,
So that they saw not the boat where it lay concealed in the willows,
And undisturbed by the dash of their oars and unseen were the
      sleepers;
Angel of God was there none to awaken the slumbering maiden!
Swiftly they glided away like the shade of a cloud on the prairie.

I can never forget the beauty of this day on the Mississippi,
and we were so unprepared for it that we enjoyed it doubly.
Certainly, we saw it under its most favourable aspect; the day
was so dreamily lovely that a mystic poetic charm seemed to
hang over everything, and it was all so thoroughly wild, the
solitude only broken by the soaring eagle, sailing away over
the tops of the bluffs as our steamer appeared. How I longed
to follow his example, only to have one glimpse of the prairie
which stretches away from the summits of the bluffs—the
prairie that I had read of and heard described a thousand
times, but never seen. We stopped only once or twice at small
settlements, or at a "wood-pile" on a solitary island, to take in
fuel for our furnaces. As we bumped against one of the islands where there was a great wood-pile, one of the men was
startled by a large snake, which had been lying curled up and
darted off from the sticks as he was lifting. We hardly left
our places in the bow: it was so enjoyable, something to remember always. All this part of the river is infinitely finer than
the Rhine, and more lovely than the Hudson, though the hills
rise higher and with greater grandeur in places on the banks
of the latter.

There is another ball going on in the saloon this evening,

but the deck is too delightful to desert it. The most extraordinary thing is how, in the darkness, they make out the channel; it changes from one side to the other every few yards almost, and yet we only ran ashore two or three times. Sometimes we seemed to float with the current, the noise of the engine ceasing entirely. The steamer was exactly like a great monster, subject to queer mysterious fits; he came to with a slight sigh, then a heavy breath, then breathed very hard for a little while, when off he went again into a state of coma.

October 1st—Another morning passed amid scenes quite as beautiful as yesterday, the hills and rocky bluffs only varying in wild picturesqueness and wonderful colouring. The leaves of the Virginia creeper and the sumach are, at this time, a brighter scarlet than at any other and the rocks are covered with them. All the way from St. Paul we have seen numbers of seagulls, although over 1,000 miles from the sea-coast. We still see a few fish-eagles hovering over the bluffs and, in the early morning, flocks of wild-ducks constantly rise from the network of lagoons which lie around the innumerable islands on our left. But we are getting into a much more thickly-settled country and stop very often. Our principal cargo besides flour seems to be the household furniture of families moving. It is so extraordinary the way people here are always changing their residence. We run up to the shore where, on the muddy bank, are lying two or three heaps of beds, bedsteads, chairs, tables, kitchen dressers, stoves, babies' perambulators, etc.; the crew carry them in to the lower deck, and then carry out two or three more collections exactly similar and off we go.

There are two barges now fastened on each side of the steamer, both full of cargo, and our gaunt Captain is in great spirits, saying it is the best trip he has made. The river has become immensely wide. At Dubuque it is spanned by a beautiful iron railway-bridge. The middle part swings open on a pivot placed in the centre pier, so that large boats may pass through. A steep cliff rises close to the water's edge and the railway runs on to the bridge, from out of a dark tunnel. Our enormous boat with its barges had just dropped through the bridge, which had not yet swung back into its proper place and was still gaping wide open, when we heard a shrill whistle in the tunnel and a train rushed out full-speed on to the bridge. Its fate seemed inevitable. A thrill of horror passed over me, and I closed my eyes not to see the terrific crash, but, when I opened them, to my astonishment the train was standing perfectly still, close to the brink to be sure, but not over! The wonderful air-brake had brought it up in an instant. We had been astonished at its action often before. Once we had met a train coming towards us on the same line, but both trains were stopped in a moment. Often from the unfenced state of the lines cattle stray on to the rails; if any are killed, the Railway has to pay for them; but this does not often happen, and I have many times seen the train pull up quite suddenly and cattle walk off very leisurely from the track; but the Railway people say calves are the most troublesome animals, for they delight in running along the track in front of the train. It is incomprehensible that the English Railways do not adopt this brake. One hardly ever hears of collisions here, such as have been startling us in England for the last year. The favourite accident here, apparently, is a train being "ditched," as the newspapers call it; that is, getting off the metals and falling over into the ditch.

Dubuque

We remained at Dubuque two or three hours, landing our 1,000 barrels of flour, and also an immense number of large paper-bags full of flour. These paper-bags are a new invention, and they are also making paper-barrels from the stalks and refuse of flax. Dubuque is a large, growing city, with valuable lead-mines near it. It is named after one of the first pioneers of the West, a Frenchman, as his name implies. He was *fanatico* upon the horrors of being buried in the earth and, in compliance with his wishes, his body was exposed in an open sepulchre on the top of the hill under which our steamer had stopped. They say that only a few years since his bones were still to be seen there, although a city bearing his name had sprung up near them.

We find that with all these delays we shall not arrive until midnight at Clinton, where we take the train for the West. I don't think we shall be sorry to leave the steamer now that we have passed the most beautiful part of the river: a very rough set of passengers have been coming in to-day, and the expectoration is really something unbearable; one has to pick one's steps about the decks with the greatest care. In the Eastern States it is only the lowest class that indulges in this horrid habit; no one who pretends to be a gentleman would dare to be guilty of such an atrocity; but here one sees nice lady-like-looking women travelling with men who are, evidently, "most prominent citizens," but who never cease chewing and "expectorating" in the most disgusting manner.

We took in a number of kegs of gunpowder at Dubuque; it was rather amusing, though one could not help feeling slightly nervous to see the nonchalant way it was treated. At first the kegs were left lying about on the deck just where they were taken in, and I saw a man sitting on one smoking a pipe! Then the Captain ordered them to be put in the hold where they would be safer, but the hatch of the hold was left open and, close to it, was the stand where the brazier of coals was put when we stopped after dark, the sparks flying in every direction!

Clinton

October 2nd—The ball was very crowded last night and was just waning when we reached Clinton. All the lower part of the saloon was filled with stands for berths where rough-looking men were sleeping—three, one above the other. There were a number of roughs hanging about the landing-place, looking anything but pleasant in the red wavering light of the pine faggots. I begged John to be careful of my bag which he had in his hand. A swaggering "Westerny"-looking man with high boots and a pistol in his belt overheard me, and turned to me saying, "If I'd have thought there was anything worth hav-

ing in it I'd have sloped with it long ago!" "Wal, I guess he
would," said the Freight-agent who was getting out our luggage for us, "Why, there was a lot of fellows here last week,
and they just hustled a passenger out in the dark over there,
and they knocked him about, robbed him of every cent he had,
and then left him there more dead than alive, I can tell you!"
I am happy to say they were not so unkind to us, but I was
much more comfortable when we got away from them and
made our way to a nice little hotel in the town, where we got
a few hours of sleep before starting on our long day's journey
to Omaha, made very fatiguing by having to travel in the ordinary car; the bad air and uncomfortable seats are a great contrast to the Pullman cars, but these last only run on the
through trains. The car we were in had a number of Bibles in
it; over every two seats was a little box with a Bible stuck in it,
and I noticed a great many people reading them. There is
really a very deep religious feeling in this country, but the
habit that a great many Americans have of speaking irrever-
ently of religion and the Bible, and of not going to Church,
shocks one very much after being accustomed to the quiet respect shown to religious subjects in England. In England an
unbeliever would hardly dare express his opinion, for if it was
generally known it would affect his social position amongst
his neighbours to such a degree that he would be almost an
outcast, and, for this reason and also out of respect for their
feelings, he will even go to Church regularly; but in America
many people speak and behave about religious matters in a
light, flippant manner that often leads English people to think
them utterly without religion. But this is a great mistake; it is

a deplorable habit, but it is only on the surface, and deeper
down there is a strong love of God. It is the same thing in
their manner of treating the aged, who are dearly loved and
cherished, but not treated with respect. It comes, I think, from
a total want of reverence in the American character, which
begins when they are children. If any children can be called
detestable, certainly American children are so, but, poor little
things, it is not their fault. Never were children so utterly
spoilt and allowed to have their own way so entirely. Of
course, when they are not taught obedience and respect for
their elders, they naturally become the rude, noisy, independ-
ent little imps that one sees running-riot in the hotel corridors
and stuffing sweets and fruit all day long in the cars until, towards evening, they have arrived at that stage of crossness and
indigestion that no amount of lollipops will pacify them, and
the air is filled with whines and cries. But think what journeys
the poor little creatures are perpetually dragged.

Omaha

As we arrived in Omaha this evening we were obliged to
change cars to cross the river, and we got into one where there
were three or four families from Indiana moving to Oregon.
There were about twelve little children amongst them, and
these people had been travelling for three days and nights,
and expected to travel twelve more days and nights, on second-
class trains, before they reached their destination. It was said

at Omaha that a fresh lot of mosquitoes came in to taste the foreign delicacies.

Colonel Dodge met us at the train at Omaha and took Mr. Blackmore off to the barracks, and we went to the hotel, where they at first declared there was not a room of any sort for us or even beds, as the great State Fair was going on in the town. However, it is a good thing to know in this great Republican country that, no matter how full the hotels are, they almost always keep one room, and that always the best, in case some particularly great swell should arrive unexpectedly, and we managed to impress the man at the office with an idea of our great importance, and he let us have this one room, much to the disgust of some people who came in with us, who evidently looked upon us as interlopers of the worst description.

This ought to be a red-letter day in my diary, for, to-day, my eyes beheld for the first time the prairie! I am sorry to say I was disappointed, but then it was not the real original prairie, but a settled, planted, and cropped prairie with only here and there a reach of a few hundred acres left in its wild state.

October 3rd—At breakfast this morning I looked around and saw Lord Claud Hamilton coming in to the room. In all our travels, so far, he is the first person we have met that we had ever seen before. He is on his way to San Francisco and the Yosemite Valley. We tried to persuade him to come with us on our buffalo hunt, but he was eager to get on to see the Yosemite, as the season is getting late.

I was just going to say there is absolutely nothing whatever to see in Omaha, when I was called to the window to see a couple of good-sized houses rambling down the street, which really is a most curious sight. They move the largest wooden houses here from one place to another on rollers, and they are quite as good as ever, after having walked from one end of the town to the other. The "Omahawks" (as the inhabitants are called) seem a very sickly-looking set, and they say the town is very unhealthy. It stands on one side of the Missouri River, with Council Bluffs—a rival town—on the opposite bank: the river rolls between them, a dark yellow muddy stream, as some one describes it, much too thick to swim in and not quite thick enough to walk on. For the first time we begin to see the frontiersmen riding about in fringed leather leggings on rough-looking horses. The Fair has brought these people into Omaha from great distances. We have just been in a shop where all sorts of Indian things are sold. They showed me a scalp, just as it was taken from the head; it had long grey hair and was most horrible. Mr. Blackmore bought a white buffalo robe, which is a great curiosity, and is valued immensely by the Indians. They look upon it with a sort of superstitious rever-ence and consider it "Great Medicine." This one was beauti-fully ornamented with porcupine quills, and the inside has all sorts of painted designs. The shop was filled with very pretty Chinese things brought from San Francisco.

John went to see General Ord, who commands this district under General Sheridan, and General Sheridan has most kindly written to him to do what he can for us. It seems there has been a dreadful scourge of grasshoppers in Nebraska; for several years in succession they have entirely devoured the crops of the settlers on the frontier, leaving not even a blade of grass behind them. These poor people are reduced to the greatest poverty and distress, and General Ord has ordered several troops—or rather companies (as they are called here) —of cavalry to hunt and kill buffalo, giving the meat to the sufferers, and he proposes that we shall do the same with the buffalo killed by our party, if we ever approach near enough to the settlements, but they seem to think that doubtful, and if we go where Sheridan advises us to, the Republican Valley, we shall be a long distance from any ranches.

October 4th—Left Omaha at noon for the West, very comfortable in a drawing-room compartment. We heard a story of an English gentleman travelling in a Pullman car, who carelessly left his purse on his bed, by the side of his gun-case, while he went out to dine; when he returned his purse was gone. He called the conductor of the car and told him his purse had been stolen. The conductor said he could do nothing and was rather insolent about it. The Englishman then thought he would look into his gun-case to see if it was all right. He began opening it: as he did so the conductor turned deadly pale and exclaimed, "Oh, Mr. ———, wait a moment, I'll look for it," put his hand under the pillow, and pulled it out. He thought our friend was getting his gun out to shoot him! Major Woolcot, the United States Marshal, was introduced to us, a functionary who performs somewhat the duties of a Sheriff, at Cheyenne. He was going "bird-shooting" on the Platte River, and seemed devoted to sport. Living at Cheyenne, he says he gets too much "big game," that is, buffalo, elk, antelope, etc., and much prefers bird-shooting. He was going out with a party of friends, and they expected to get 200 to 300 head of game a day, principally wild duck and teal, wild geese, brandt and prairie-chicken.

The Prairie

Soon after leaving Omaha we saw the dreadful havoc committed by the locusts; wherever there was the least cultivation around the settlers' houses, only the bare yellow stalks of the corn were left; but very soon we left all settlements behind us, and our single line of rails ran straightly over the level country as far as one could see, until lost in the distance. On each side the yellow, treeless prairie, like a great ocean with great yellow waves, stretched away without a landmark of any sort, not even a bush or shrub, only the short yellow buffalo-grass. It is only now that the peculiar qualities of this grass are being found out; apparently, it is only a burnt-up tuft of grass, but the heart of every tuft is green and completely buried in a fringe of dried grass, which is like well-cured hay. In the spring it grows long and luxuriantly; then comes the long dry summer, and the peculiar atmosphere has this effect upon the grass. Animal fatten upon it in the most marvellous manner. They say it would suit sheep better even than cattle, but, as yet, very few have been tried on it. This great tract of land, extending from the Missouri River to the Rocky Mountains, was formerly called "The Great American Desert," and was supposed to be perfectly sterile; but now it is becoming every year more and more covered with enormous herds of cattle, wherever there is water for them. The solitary monotony of the scene we are passing through is almost as depressing as when we ran for a day through the dim, endless Michigan forests. There is an odd-looking old Quaker in the car, an Indian Commissioner, 75 years old; he wears a chintz dressing-gown and silky wig. He is going from Maine, on the Atlantic coast, to Oregon, on the Pacific, to settle some Indian troubles.

As evening drew on Colonel Dodge (who had come with us from Omaha) kept us enthralled with wild, thrilling stories of the scenes enacted here during the making of this Railway, which the Indians had determined they would not allow to be made. The first trains that ran were continually stopped by Indians, and it is only since they have stationed military Posts all along the line that the attacks have ceased. It was dusk when we passed through Julesberg, celebrated two or three years ago as the scene of the greatest atrocities of frontier life. It was the refuge of the roughest of the rough, where everybody's pistol was carried at full-cock, and over two hundred graves were made in the burial ground before anybody had died a natural death!

Sydney Barracks

October 5th—At eight this morning we arrived at Sydney Barracks, a military Post on the plains about 200 miles from the Rocky Mountains. As the train drew near, the Post looked like

an oasis in the desert, with its rows of young green cotton-
wood trees and neat houses; an irrigating ditch around the
Post enabled the officers to cultivate nice little gardens. About
four acres, altogether, are enclosed with a low palisade; all
outside is the boundless prairie.

We found General Morrow waiting for us at the station,
with an ambulance and four white mules to take us the short
distance to his quarters. I never saw four such fat mules, and
one of the officers told me with great pride, that they were the
same mules which had drawn Duke Alexis—"the young
Russ"—when he went out buffalo-hunting. General Morrow
has most kindly arranged everything for our hunting party.
We are to have every luxury, plenty of horses and tents, a good
cook, and a servant or two, an ambulance for us when we are
tired of riding, and a large escort of cavalry to take care of us.
They are glad to give this sort of duty to the troops; it accus-
toms them to bivouacking and they like it beyond everything.
I find General Morrow was with my dear father[4] when he was
mortally wounded at the battle of the Wilderness in Virginia;
he commanded a brigade in my father's Division, and was
himself wounded in the same action. General Morrow was in-
spired with the same devotion to him personally that everyone
who came in contact with him felt; it was his noble self-sacri-
ficing character and great bravery. General Morrow told me of
one instance of his, perhaps, too-reckless bravery and disre-
gard of his own personal safety, which occurred at one of the
battles of Fredericksburg. My father's Division was ordered to
cross the Rappahannock River, on the opposite side of which

[4] General Wadsworth.

the rebels had a line of rifle-pits. A part of General Morrow's regiment was ordered to cross in small boats, to dislodge these sharpshooters, so that the bridges could be made. They had attempted the passage several times, but had always been driven back. My father, who was watching their movements from a distance, at last became impatient, and rode down to the bank urging the men to make another attempt. The boats put off, but half-way across a terrific fire was opened upon them; several men fell and again they wavered. My father, who had jumped into a boat that was just starting, and was leading his swimming horse behind him, came up at that moment, crying "Forward! Forward!" which so inspirited the men that they pushed rapidly on, the soldiers helping the rowers with the butts of their muskets. They landed, rushed up the banks, and in a few minutes, had driven the riflemen from their pits, capturing some of them. My father rode up to them, his horse still dripping and called out in great delight, "God bless you, men of the 24th." From that day those words became the rallying-cry of the regiment, and in many a fierce struggle General Morrow has heard them shout out, as they rushed impetuously on, "God bless you, men of the 24th!"

It has been raining all day, apparently much to everybody's astonishment, for it is generally supposed that when once the dry autumn sets in on the Plains there is no rain, a snowstorm opening the winter season at the end of October or beginning of November; but they apologize for this rainy day by saying, that now the Railway across the plains has made changes in the climate! Professor Agassiz is actually given as an authority! and the theory is, that the current of air caused by the quick rushing of the trains has some magnetic influence; but it certainly is true that, wherever the railway has been made, there is more rain and there are more storms than formerly. We have just heard that an immense band of Sioux Indians are encamped about 30 miles from here; they are hunting buffalo for their winter supply of meat. They are very anxious to be on good terms with the military so that their hunting may not be interfered with, for without the buffalo in winter they starve. A few herds of buffalo, they say, have just appeared in this neighbourhood on their way South.

October 6th—At breakfast this morning we heard the news that the principal Chief of the Indians encamped near here— "Two-Lance"—has come in with an interpreter to signify his friendly intentions, which is pleasant for us to hear, as we are going in the direction of his camp. We found old "Two-Lance" a natural gentleman, but cunning and cruelty were said to be his special characteristics. He reports the buffalo in great numbers close to them. Yesterday, 300 of his young "Braves" had a great buffalo "surround." They encircled a herd of 125 buffalo and gradually closed in upon them, killing nearly every one. After breakfast a council was held with "Two-Lance," and he made a speech which the interpreter—a half-breed—put into very good English. First of all they smoked the pipes of peace, which he brought with him and handed around from one to the other. After the council General Morrow brought him to see me; I went out to the porch to receive him and we shook hands: his felt so singular—soft and small —the long, thin, slight fingers, like the soft, hairy paw of an animal. All the Indian men have these delicate hands, they never do any work whatever, leaving it all to the squaws; their feet are also small and curiously turned-in. The Chief was dressed in leather shirt and leggings beautifully-embroidered in beads, having a handsome dark-blue blanket thrown around him. His face, with a fringe of tangled black hair falling over it, looked very old and weather-beaten, and a grey wide-awake hat, with "Two-Lance" painted in big letters on the band, completed his dress. We asked him into the drawing-room, where he was completely at his ease. He sat down on a chair and placed his long pipe at his feet and, for a few minutes, sat quite immovable, his head thrown back, only his eyes roaming about, taking in me and everything else in the room, and then began in his soft, low voice, making pretty speeches to me, which the interpreter translated. They had told him I was the daughter of a great Chief, and he said the squaws would load me with trophies when we visited their camp, and what an honour it would be for them receiving us; and that he was anxious to hurry home and tell his people that we were going to visit them, and to see that the dogs were killed, and other animals so as to prepare a great feast for us. "The dogs and other animals!" (At a dog-feast we actually saw the skin!) Every now and then he got up and shook hands violently with me, saying, "How-How," which meant simply that he wished to be civil. All at once he became very fidgety and uneasy— poor man—he wished to "expectorate." He got up, looked all around the room for a "spittoon" and, not seeing anything that looked like one, and being much too civil to deface Mrs. Morrow's pretty carpet, he at last, in a fit of desperation, held

out his own hand and used it as a "spittoon!" It was rather an
extraordinary proceeding, but I positively thought it more gen-
tleman-like than the way our friends on the Mississippi steamboat sent volleys of tobacco-juice all day over the beautiful vel-
vet carpets. I noticed with joy that it was the left hand, fortunately, not the one he insisted on shaking hands with. He
promised to arrange a great "surround" for us, so that we
should see the way the Indians hunt buffalo, and also to get up
a war-dance if they can collect enough warriors, but he says
many of them will be away at great distances hunting. He had
with him an Indian boy, who squatted on the ground and kept
his little sharp black eyes fixed upon me with the most intense
curiosity. When he left I accompanied him to the door and
saw him walk off, not a very imposing sight, as all these Indians are so absolutely bow-legged from always riding.

Mr. Blackmore has bought a quantity of things from the
Quarter-master's stores here, to take to them as presents—
bright-coloured blankets and shirts, small mirrors and sugar
and coffee, also some boxes of "hard-tack," the hard biscuits
made for the soldiers, which the Indians prize immensely.
This afternoon the fog cleared and we went out for a ride, as I
wanted to try the horse they have selected for me, a charming
little chestnut, I am delighted with him. He has a good mouth,
a nice canter, and he ambles, which is a delightful pace for
long journeys; one can ride all day without feeling tired. What
a piece of luck finding such a good horse. We enjoyed our
ride on the prairie and had several gallops after jack rabbits, a
sort of hare, larger but not so fast. We met two rough-looking
characters riding Indian ponies, suggestive-looking figures in

red shirts with guns slung behind them. We start early to-morrow and I am very busy arranging my outfit; buttons and strings must all be in their places for the next fortnight's work. In the evening several of the officers and their wives came in to General Morrow's. Some of them have been through great hardships in this frontier life, being constantly moved from one Fort or Post to another during the heat of summer, or the terrible cold of the winter. I believe they all look upon me as quite a lunatic to think of camping-out and living in tents for pleasure; and, above all, riding all day. Very few of these ladies ride or, indeed, try to amuse themselves in any way, and life at these Frontier Posts must be very dull work, though it seems very much the fault of the officers themselves, for there is sport of one kind or another to be had at nearly all these Forts, but they do not avail themselves of it. At one of the Forts in Arizona there is a young Irishman—Captain Coppinger—who has got up a pack of hounds and hunts jack rabbits; but at Sydney and other Forts, though antelope were constantly within reach, and the prairie afforded such capital riding, the officers seemed to prefer hanging about the Post.

October 7th—We were enjoined most particularly last night to be sure and be ready at seven this morning to make an early start. I was in such a state of excitement that I was up, dressed and all packed long before; but it was nine o'clock before even the waggons with the tents and all the heavy paraphernalia got off, and nearly ten when the ambulance stopped in front of General Morrow's door to take in all our odds and ends in the way of handbags, cloaks and rugs, etc. The word ambulance

does not give the least idea of the cheerful-looking vehicle
called by that name, which had first met us at the station when
we arrived at Sydney, and is now to accompany us across the
prairie as a refuge for any of us who get tired of riding. It is
painted bright-green, has a white-canvas top and sides, and is
drawn by four white mules with scarlet collars, driven by a
soldier in the light-blue U.S. uniform. It is very roomy inside,
with seats for four; the backs of the seats are movable, so that
they can be made into a bed. All our bags, etc., were stowed
inside, also a large lunch-basket; two or three extra guns and
rifles were placed in the bottom; by their side the precious umbrella, in its shining case in which it had been brought tenderly
and carefully all the way from Queenstown, was gently laid
carefully protected from the rough onslaught of any rude
cartridge-case or gun-barrel. Colonel Dodge's dog— "Bunkum," a brown retriever with a most extraordinary double nose,
which they say is the peculiarity of a Russian breed of dogs—
then perched himself gravely on the back seat. "Dave," the
negro factotum, sat opposite to him. The driver, an Irishman
named Lynch, flourished his whip over the mules' ears, and
they all four started off with a jerk at full gallop. "Bunkum"
and "Dave" were flung violently into each other's arms; there
was a dreadful tumble and crash of handbags and baskets and
a rattle of iron underneath, which made the owner of the
loved umbrella turn pale: but they were off, which was a comfort and one step towards a start, so it now only remained to
get ourselves and our escort fairly under way also; but this
was not so easy. The Captain of our escort declared that he had
not eaten anything for twenty-four hours and must have a cup

of coffee before starting. The brim of my low felt hat was unanimously condemned, and it was predicted that I should have no skin left on my face if it was not better protected from the fierce rays of the prairie sun. General Morrow, fortunately, discovered an immense broad-brimmed hat amongst his things and kindly gave it to me. English saddles and saddle-girths seem very simple things but it was half-an-hour before we could get ours properly put on and, twice after I mounted, my chestnut pirouetting a little, the saddle turned with me before I got away from the door, which was great "divarshun" for the command, who had all come out to see us start. Eleven o'clock, and no signs of the escort being nearly ready, so we decided to ride on and let it follow us, much to my grief, for, never before in my life having had a real escort of my own, own, own, I wished to have all the honour and glory of the thing possible, and agreed with Colonel C. that it was "very small potatoes and few in a ridge" to ride off with only an orderly apiece, instead of an imposing phalanx of fifty. Dillon is my orderly's name; he is to ride always behind me and do whatever I bid him. I begin by giving him my parasol to carry; he sticks it into his belt next to his pistol! and, as his uniform is made up of odds and ends of all sorts, it does not seem so wonderfully out-of-place as it sounds. Just as we were saying our last good-byes to Mrs. Morrow, Pallardie, who had started in the morning with the waggons, came galloping in to tell us that *"they"* had broken down while crossing a little creek only two miles from the Post: a bad beginning, and we hastened on to see how matters really stood. Poor Pallardie had passed the previous night at the saloons in Sydney, preparing and strengthening himself for the privations he was to endure, and the Doctor had warned Colonel Dodge that it was just touch-and-go whether he would have D.T. or not. We soon found the waggons; one of them only had broken down and its contents were scattered all over the bed of the creek. The waggons were all very heavily laden and there were only four mules to each, not enough, considering the heavy ground we were going over. The one that had broken down contained the forage for our horses. We expect to make long marches and, if we meet buffalo, they must be in condition for galloping. Colonel Dodge left directions as to what was to be done and we trotted on.

The morning was most beautiful, and the clear delicious air put us all in the highest spirits; and then the intense, delightful excitement of starting on such a novel expedition, not knowing what adventures we may have; our spirited little horses bounding under us, enjoying it as much as we did; the great prairies all before us rolling away in wave after wave, the most perfect ground for riding. A few miles only from the Fort we came upon the carcasses of buffalo, some whitened from two or three years' exposure and the others quite fresh, and we were never out of sight of them. For the first six miles we cantered quickly on, General Morrow accompanying us; then we had a sensation. There was a cry of "antelope," and, in the distance where the ground rose a little, we descried five or six faint shadowy specks on the skyline: we galloped towards them, but, before we were near enough for them even to take a definite shape in our eyes, they perceived us and vanished as if blown away. General Morrow and two of his

A.D.C.'s bade us goodbye and left us now, to see if they could get a shot at them. Our cavalcade had become quite imposing, the ambulance following us closely, the mules trotting cheerily over the perfectly-smooth prairie, "Bunkum" and "Dave" nodding at each other inside. Our guide and Indian interpreter heads the procession to show us the way; his hat is gaily decorated with ribbons and with a scarlet handkerchief round his throat, and his belt stuck full of knives, pistols and cartridges: in the distance he looks very picturesque, but his face and the limp way he sits his horse tell a tale of the Sydney saloons, and he soon came to grief; his horse put his foot in a badger-hole and tumbled him over. It was a very soft place but he declared he was utterly killed and lay prone on the ground, invoking all his saints, a long list of them. At last he was persuaded to get into the ambulance, and a glass of whisky made him all right again. We now saw herds of antelope every two or three miles, but all at a great distance.

Colonel Dodge is considered the great "shottist" of the great West, and I was very anxious to see him perform. We were riding together when we saw a herd flying away from us at a few hundred yards. He quickly dismounted, and I held his horse while he took steady aim; the first shot only sent them flying faster away but, at the second, one of them stopped, and, to my amazement, after standing for a few moments, fell over; the distance was about 400 yards. Mr. Blackmore was anxious to get to the Indians this evening, and it was settled that he should take Pallardie with him and make for their camp, where he would sleep. Before he left us we stopped and rested for an hour to take our luncheon. The sun was very hot, but we sat in the shade of the ambulance; some most comfortable camp chairs had been put in at the last moment, and *such* a lunch! though the prairie air is so sustaining that food seems quite a superfluity. We were to go on for about ten miles to a "divide" which Pallardie showed us in the distance, and where he assured us we should find water, by the side of which we were to make our camp. The afternoon was hot and I was glad of my broad-brimmed hat. Although the prairie stretched away monotonously on all sides, at every moment some new object of interest was presented to us. Now it was a flock of huge grey birds soaring slowly above us; we had never seen anything like them and found they were sand-cranes, an immense bird and, when standing, six feet high. Then a prairie-dog town was the next excitement, and when one first sees these ridiculous little creatures standing on top of their holes, barking and stroking their noses with their paws, then suddenly bolting down their holes with a furious wag of their tails, it is the most ludicrous little game!

We had gone on for hours, had crossed Pallardie's "divide" and, looking in every direction, saw no signs of water and were beginning to feel rather anxious, knowing the state Pallardie was in, when, as we were riding along the bed of a small creek, a large buffalo bull appeared suddenly on the bluff over our heads. Our first buffalo! The yellow grass of the prairie was all so light in the fierce glare of the sun that, as I looked up suddenly and saw this great dark mass, he seemed supernaturally black and immense; but, of course, one's first buffalo ought to look very big. As soon as he saw us, he turned and galloped off and, as he disappeared over the bluff, we discovered that one of his hind legs was broken and dangled in the air! John galloped after it "to put the poor animal out of its pain," but it had rather a start on the other side of the bluff, and, when he came in sight of it, was miles away. We still went on looking for water, crossing one "divide" after another, but in vain, and as the sun began to set and our horses to flag as well as ourselves, and there was no prospect of camp, things did not look quite so bright; but still, to me, it was all so exciting and so novel that I felt sure I could ride all night; the very idea of searching for water was perfectly thrilling! In every book of travel one has ever read, does not the traveller pass through extraordinary adventures? But our adventures were all nipped in the bud by our simultaneous discovery of a large pool of rain-water in the sand at the foot of a slight hill, and here I am sitting by its side, while everybody about me is busy arranging for the night, that is, as well as they can arrange, for our waggons, with tents and almost every necessary of life are miles behind us. The sun is setting in a blaze of light and colour, as, I believe, only an American sun can set. Not a tree or a bush have we in sight, only the vast stretch of rolling plain with its short yellow buffalo grass. The cavalry horses are all picketed in front of us. Most of the men are wandering about in pairs, holding between them a horse-sheet in which they are gathering "buffalo-chips" for our camp-fires, the only fuel possible here; the white mules are squealing with the pleasure of a good roll in the sand; the butcher is skinning one of the antelopes killed to-day, an operation which "Bunkum" is watching with the deepest and most searching interest; "Dave" is trying to light a fire of the buffalo-chips,

but they are so damp that, although he has been on his hands
and knees blowing it for the last ten minutes, with all the
strength of his lungs and until his eyes started out of their
sockets, yet it *will* not burn and the evening is beginning to
turn very cold.

It is nearly dark and still no signs of the waggons with all
our camp equipage, and what are we to do for dinner, and
where are we to sleep?

October 8th—I wrote until every ray of light had vanished
last night, and then was covered up with rugs and tried to
keep warm by the wretched fire. It was inconceivable that the
night could turn so bitterly cold the instant the sun had gone
down. Still no signs of the waggons with all our camp-equip-
age. We dined off the remains of hard-boiled eggs and biscuits
left in the lunch-basket, and I must say were wonderfully
cheery, but who would not be with such a raconteur of amusing stories as Colonel Dodge by one's side? and our peals of
laughter did not sound like no bed and no dinner. The soldiers
gathered round the fires, and pleasant, indeed, was the evening. As we listened to his excellent stories, in the middle of
them we heard the sound of horses galloping towards us, and
three Indians pulled up short at our camp-fire. The night was
blackest darkness and our fire very dull, so that we could only
dimly see their wild-looking figures with long streaming hair,
long blankets and beaded mocassins and leggings. They had
come from the Indian camp and brought with them Mr.
Blackmore's orderly, to tell us that he had arrived safely
amongst them, that "Two-Lance" had received him most cor-

dially and made him as comfortable as possible. He advised us to follow them to-day and camp on the opposite side of the river Platte from the Indians. We gave the Indians a note to take back to Mr. Blackmore, and I hoped they would go at once: but no, they rolled themselves in their blankets and squatted on the other side of the camp-fire, and watched us and talked about us in their low guttural voices, all the time smoking cigarettes which they rolled up themselves, pulling out long strips of cigarette-paper from their belts, each holding his pony by a long leather lariat of braided hide, so that the animal could graze, and they settled themselves, evidently for the night. About ten, the messenger we had sent back to the waggons returned, saying they had broken down again about five miles off, and that they could not possibly reach our camp before morning. The forage for the horses was the principal trouble, and it was settled that they were to leave it on the spot and bring on the waggons without it, so that, at least, we could have breakfast. And then came the question, how we were all to sleep? It was proposed that a bed should be made for me in the ambulance, and the gentlemen should make themselves comfortable and sleep on the ground around the camp-fire. I, too, was longing to sleep in the open-air, and under the stars like everyone else, to see what it was like for once in one's life, but should never have closed my eyes with those horrid Indians within sight; it was not fear, but repulsion. There was, of course, no danger: but the very idea of knowing that their dreadful wicked faces were there would have prevented one's sleeping. As it was, after a most comfortable bed had been made inside the ambulance, and the white-canvas curtains were drawn down all round, I could not even think of sleeping; everything was so novel, so exciting; every now and then the shrill, prolonged dismal cry of the coyote (a small wolf) came out of some far solitude, ringing through the silent air, and making one shiver with that vague sense of evil near that one has sometimes. Then the mules, which were hobbled, would come whinnying about the ambulance, rattling their chains. There was a little wind, too, which whistled through the curtains and, as the night grew brighter towards morning, I could not resist watching the weird scene outside—the sleeping figures scattered in every direction, and the dim camp-fire of buffalo chips, with the crouching figures of the Indians still holding their ponies. One of the waggons came in in the night, which made a great commotion.

About daybreak an orderly rode in from Sydney with a letter from General Morrow to say that he had received orders to go to Louisiana on Saturday, and asking us to send back David, the negro servant, to help him pack up. This was a great blow to us, for so much of our comfort depended upon him; however, one of the troopers named Reddie was detailed for this duty, and I dare say we shall get on very well. "Dave" is in despair at not going on with us, and evidently thinks himself made for heroic deeds.

I was really tired in the morning, my long ride of the day before and want of sleep began to tell, but when the waggons came in the mess things were got out, and a delicious breakfast of antelope liver, coffee and hot rolls, made one feel ready for anything again. The cooking apparatus amused me very much at first: it was exactly like a small iron bedstead; when the fire was made it was put on top of it, and a row of pots and kettles replaced the mattress; it was certainly a capital contrivance. The poor troopers had had nothing to eat since they had left the Post the morning before, and all their food was in the waggons, which they were glad enough to see come in. We were not able to start until twelve, there were so many delays in the arrival of the waggons, but I passed a delightful morning sitting lazily in a camp-chair in the shade of the ambulance. Numerous herds of antelope, timidly browsing, came over the top of the hill towards the pool for their morning drink, very much astonished to see it surrounded by intruders. Some came quite close and many shots were fired at them, but none were hit. One little herd of five or six quite lost their heads, and, after circling around once or twice, dashed almost through the camp. Colonel Dodge told us a story of a friend of his who was fond of boasting of his extraordinary shots, and one day at dinner he was telling his friends that he had shot an antelope at 500 yards, and the bullet went through his foot and his head; his friends pooh-poohed the idea— impossible: such a thing couldn't happen. "Now, Sam," turning to his negro servant, "isn't that true? Didn't I shoot that antelope right through both the head and the foot?" "Yes, Massa, dats as true as I am a black nigger—de animal was just a-scratching his head with his hind-foot and your bullet, Massa, just nailed 'em right together! But, Massa, please," (in a whisper) "jis put 'em a little closer togedder next time— dat was terrible hard work!"

The River Platte

At last we made a start, and this time the whole cortège started together, and what with the troop of soldiers, waggons and ambulance, headed by ourselves and our orderlies, I thought it was truly imposing. We rode towards the river Platte, crossing some large prairie-dog villages, where our party had some good shots at these funny little animals, with their tails wagging incessantly. We soon came in sight of the Platte, miles away, but in this wonderful atmosphere we could see it as clearly as possible, winding like a broad ribbon through the wide yellow treeless plain, not even the smallest bush visible to make a shadow on its banks—truly called the Platte—from half-a-mile to nearly a mile in breadth, very shallow and fordable almost everywhere, excepting for the numerous quicksands, filled with islands where the black-tailed deer lie concealed in the long grass and tangled growth. The old emigrant trail from the Eastern States to the Rocky Mountains followed the banks of this river, and, I suppose, almost every portion of the banks has been camped upon: and what charming spots for a camp! such beautiful grass; and such brilliant fresh-looking water. We soon came upon the old trail, now so little used, with the deep ruts made by the heavy waggons.

About three o'clock we saw far before us a group of figures on horseback, magnified by the mirage into wonderful giants on impossible long-legged horses; sometimes the legs were quite detached from the ground, and they seemed to be moving just above the cantle. As we approached we discovered that it was our friend, Mr. Blackmore, with Pallardie and a number of Indians coming to meet us. The old chief—"Two-Lance"—rode[5] foremost and with his son, a nice little fellow of twelve, but hideously painted, called "The Brave Boy," and there were some other Chiefs, their dress a strange mixture of the really picturesque Indian costume and odds and ends from civilization, which they had donned in our honour. Poor old "Two-Lance" wore his richly-embroidered buck-skin leggings and deep necklace of wampum, with an old Captain's uniform coat and a broad-brimmed felt hat tied under his chin by a white cotton pocket-handkerchief. Another of the Braves had a splendidly-embroidered scarlet Indian blanket thrown over his shoulders and, on his head, an old U.S. Cavalry helmet coming half-way down over his queer yellow-ochre painted face, but *all* had their rifles slung across their saddles in front of them, and belts filled with cartridges round their bodies, with a few pistols and knives peeping out here and there. "Two-Lance" was very civil and very careful in showing his boy how to be civil and shake hands properly with all of us.

The Indian Lodges

We all rode on together and very soon came in sight of the Indian Lodges on the opposite side of the river. The air was filled with the noise of the Indian camp opposite—children

[5] The Indians had some wild horses—mustangs—that they had caught recently, but few remain in this part. These mustangs can never be tamed, though they will go on quietly for months.

shouting, dogs barking, and every now and then drums beating. The children are never flogged. Their punishment for faults is to have their faces painted black and to be turned out of the Lodge, with nothing to eat for a day. Pallardie—who had lived amongst the Indians and had had two or three squaws as wives, but now had left them and married a white woman—told us how the little boys from 12 to 16 had been having a sham fight, to teach them how to meet their enemies. They assemble and form two camps opposite each other. They are quite naked, as usual, but on their heads is fastened a little tuft of grass, and they wear a belt in which a wooden knife is stuck. They are armed with bows, and arrows made of some soft substance that will not hurt. The signal is given and, in an instant, the battle begins. When any one of them is hit by an arrow he falls down as if dead and his enemy rushes up to him, pulls out his wooden knife, and tears off the tuft of grass on the scalp, rushing off again at once to avoid being caught by one of the others.

The mirage magnified the Lodges and drew them up to a fabulous height, so that they seemed towering into the skies. No one can believe until they have seen it, what the mirage will do on these plains. At a little distance a crow looks like a man hopping about, and a man is drawn out until he seems twenty feet high! All around the Indian encampment were enormous droves of ponies: the scene was really imposing. Pallardie told me they had 7,000 which, I suppose, may mean 3,000 or 4,000, but they seemed countless.

We chose a charming grassy spot for our camp opposite the Indians, and made arrangements to cross the river to visit them immediately, but, while we were resting for half-an-hour and enjoying a cup of tea, Mrs. Two-Lance came over to call upon me. She rode up to our tent sitting on a man's saddle, but quite at her ease, as a Queen should be; all the squaws ride in this way. She is a young, very pleasant-looking woman, with the filthiest old short calico petticoat on, a very smart modern striped shawl, and leather leggings and mocassins most beautifully and richly embroidered with beads. I never saw such beautiful bead-work, very pretty shades of blue predominated. The Indians watch me as an object of the greatest wonder and curiosity, to see any woman treated with respect and consideration. Mrs. Two-Lance was greatly surprised when her tea-spoon was picked up for her.

It is all like a dream, it seems too strange to be true, that I should see these uncivilized Indians now really for the first time in my life, when I return to America almost as a foreigner. I remember all the traditions of Indians that used to be told us children at Geneseo, of the battles that were fought there by the first settlers, of the great tree where they used to hold councils: how we used to scan the floor of the old "Homestead" for the marks of the Indian mocassins which were made when they came in with wet feet to hold councils with my grandfather: how imagination used to run riot in dwelling on these strange wild creatures. And here we were surrounded by them in all their paint and feathers and leather and bead-work, their wicked faces glaring at us from all directions. All the lands of the Indians have been purchased by Government, and the Indians are paid annually in provisions and blankets, instead of being paid in one large sum: one dollar in ten

reaches them! We heard, too accounts of the state of affairs
in the "Indian Department"—of the fortunes that are made
—how Indians are swindled and starved—how shoddy blankets are sold to them—how badly "appropriations" are dis-
pensed—of commissions being granted to private individuals
before the appropriation reaches the Indians; but such is the
power of the Indian Department in Congress, that no attempt
to put a stop to it has succeeded: twenty millions a-year are
disbursed.

The Indians, most of them had a half-derisive expression
on their countenances, anything but reassuring. They all wear
their hair parted in the middle and hanging in a tangled mass
at each side, the ends braided, and, as it is considered a beauty
to have it long, there are bits of fur and tails of animals hanging down in front. They have a strict code of manners: one of
their rules is to argue, but never dispute, and no matter how
excited and interested they are they never interrupt, nothing
they think worse manners.

The Chief asked us to come over and hold a council, and
said they intended to give us a great feast. They were very impatient to get us over before dark, as they had no candles. They
had intended breaking up their camp that day to leave for the
South, but waited in order to receive us. The Platte River was
nearly a mile broad at this place and was easily forded; in
fact, as soon as we arrived on our side, shoals of Indians began crossing over to us on their little ponies and squatting
down around our camp, watching everything we did: and,
presently, the little children, who were quite naked, came
wading over, and a crowd of them were just coming in, when

one of the Chiefs turned half-round and said a little word
very quietly to them, which made them turn and scamper off,
tumbling over each other. The ambulance was got ready again
and I asked Mrs. Two-Lance to return in it with me while the
gentlemen rode across. She evidently thought it a great honour,
and sat opposite to me, bouncing about on the seat with every
jolt, looking anything but comfortable: and, when we got to
the other side, she jumped out almost before we had stopped.
There was a great crowd to see us arrive: in every direction
wild peering faces, some painted all red, others yellow with
a streak of red under the eyes, and some a greenish-yellow
with dark green spots, which were most ghastly and fiendish.
The young girls, generally, knew enough of civilization to
put a dab of red somewhere on their cheeks, generally a square
or oblong patch.

The wigwams were literally swarming with children, and
yet they say the Indian race is dying. The buffalo robes being
tanned were stretched on the ground by pins in every direction,
and the stench from them and from these dirty people, dogs
and swarms of ponies, was something fearful. We proceeded
to the council-tent, put up for the occasion, fortunately for us.
One Indian stood up at the door and shouted out a long string
of names, while men crept in at the small opening. The fashionable thing was to arrive late and to be called several times.
Opposite to us "Two-Lance" and "Fire-Lightning" were
squatted in the middle of the tent. A white buffalo robe, full
of fleas, was spread for us to sit on, which we did, in a row,
the two Chiefs first having shaken hands with us, uttering a
guttural "Heaw," which is their equivalent to "how do you

do?" Gradually the tent was encircled by warriors gorgeously
got up in the pure Indian dress. The bead-work was beautiful
and the deep wampum, and the worked mother-o'-pearl neck-
laces and earrings made me quite envious. Their wampum
ornaments used to be of great value, being shells cut and filed:
but now there is a manufactory of wampum in Philadelphia
which sells immense quantities. One man appeared in great
contrast, without any ornaments, and, in fact, with no clothes
at all on but an old blanket very carefully wrapped around
him. I was told this was the fashionable way of mourning for
dead relatives and, as there had been much sickness and many
deaths, I saw numbers in the camp in this garb.

As soon as the tent was full, a squaw brought in the feast,
which consisted of a large tin basin of boiled beans, a pail
with bits of cooked meats, which might have been anything—
dogs, skunks or buffalo-meat—and large cans of tea and
coffee. We could all see that Mrs. Two-Lance took bits of meat
out of the pot, felt them to see if they were well-cooked, and
returned them. We were in a hurry to have this Pow-wow over
and to cross the river before dark, but it was difficult to make
them begin. The light grew fainter, and through the small
entrance that was the only opening in the tent we could see
the sun setting. The Chiefs sat in several rows round us. Colonel Dodge stood up and told them that we had come out to
have a buffalo-hunt and were anxious to see their mode of
killing the buffalo. We had heard that they intended having
a great surround in a few days, and we wished to know in
what direction. (A surround is managed as follows: A circle
of horsemen at equal distances apart surround the herd of

buffalo and gradually close in upon them. When they see the herd making in one direction, as they usually do, all the horsemen gallop furiously in that direction and close in upon them so thickly, and with such hideous yells, that the herd, frightened and confused, is obliged to turn and, moving off in another direction, is again met and baffled and thrown into still greater confusion, until at last the poor beasts are utterly dazed, and then the Indians find them an easy prey and kill them in hundreds, but hardly ever without suffering themselves and losing some of their horses in the press and *mêlée*, when the buffalo-bulls, wounded and infuriated, turn frantically upon the horses which are not able to get out of their way; but it always ends in the whole herd being destroyed, and then these warriors go back to their Lodges to rest after the conflict, while the squaws are sent out to skin the animals, and bring home the meat and skins—"making meat," they call it. The Indians only kill for meat and robes: white buffalo-hunters have their mode of killing: they steal up, shoot one after another of the herd, who stand stupidly and see each one fall—sometimes fifty or sixty will be killed before they take alarm. Everywhere on the ranches buffalo-meat is cut up into pieces and hung on a string to dry in the sun, which it does without spoiling, without any smoke or salt.) When he had finished speaking several Chiefs got up and spoke in turn, of course, through the interpreter who stood near us.

All the Chiefs advised us not to go, and begged us to intercede with the Great Father to stop the white buffalo-hunters, who only came to get the skins and left the flesh, which was their food, to waste. We saw the feeling was for us not to go

and, just at dark, we managed to cut short their speeches and
get away. The whole thing was exactly like the descriptions
one has read in Cooper and Catlin. The deep guttural "haugh"
they uttered whenever anything pleased them, etc. We re-
crossed the river and found the camp all settled, the mess-tent
looking very bright and cheery with the dinner-table laid and
the candles lighted, and our own tent with its comfortable
little iron bedsteads made up. One wanted to go to bed at once
to make up for the discomforts of the night before. A lot of
Indians were still squatting about the camp-fire, their hideous
faces peering out from their blankets, which they had wound
tightly around them. One of the Chiefs came over and sent
them all away before we went to bed. Our tent was a little distance from the others. Though I knew there was no real danger, I confess I was not quite happy, and woke at, I think,
every ten minutes or so all night, imagining I saw a stealthy
figure crawling in to our tent, or heard a war-whoop, and that
these horrid fierce painted faces were pouncing down upon us.
One time when I woke I was so sure that there were Indians
gathering around the tent, that I thought I would just go and
see, and I put my foot out of bed—on to an awful wild animal,
a lion or a panther at least. My shrieks aroused the whole
camp, and the harmless Indian dog, the cause of all the panic,
slunk away in the confusion. Morning came and I felt very
much ashamed of myself, but their faces were too dreadful, and
I could not help feeling impressed by them. We were entirely
in their power, for our handful of soldiers could not have
stood against such great numbers—700 or 800 Braves, all well
armed. Three years ago there were desperate fights between

these same Sioux Indians and the Whites all over the country,
but they were always defeated and have been at peace ever
since; besides, the Indians hardly ever fight at this season, that
is, never commence hostilities, for they have the long winter
before them, when it is a hard struggle for them to live at all,
and they do not wish to be disturbed.

The formal notes of the Council held on this day are interesting, and may be recorded here:

Notes of Speeches

AT A COUNCIL GIVEN BY THE CHIEFS AND BRAVES OF
THE "CUT-OFF" BAND OF OGALLALLA SIOUX,
ON THE SOUTH PLATTE, OCT. 8TH, 1874

COLONEL DODGE—"My friends, I am very glad to see you.
Some of my white friends have never seen Indians before, and
have come a long way to do so. I have known Indians for 27
years, sometimes as friends, sometimes as enemies. As for me,
I always want to be friends.

"This lady is the daughter of one of our great War-Chiefs,
killed in battle. General Sheridan sent her out to me to see
you and the buffaloes.

"When we started we did not know that you were here, but
when we were told, we thought it best at once to come and
see you, so that you may show my friends how you kill the
buffalo. One of our waggons broke down on the way, or we
should have been here before, as we wanted to be with you
before dark.

"I am very glad to see you, and I hope we shall be good
friends now and always."

MR. BLACKMORE then followed with a few remarks; after which, "FIRE-LIGHTNING" the head of the "Strong-Heart" Band, got up, and, after shaking hands with all, spoke as follows:

"We are not talking foolishly, but honestly. You and I speak truth." (Then addressing Mr. Blackmore) he said: "I see you are making notes of what we say, that you may tell our Great Father. Look at all these young men. They all behave well to the Whites; they always have done so, and they always will do so for the future.

"It makes my heart feel glad to see a lot of big men sitting down with us. I will now tell you something. Look at all my people and tell my Great Father that we had nothing to eat at the Agency, and that we have come here to hunt buffalo. We have always done so, and shall continue to do so as long as buffalo exist.

"You tell me that the Whites are good to our people. But when I look at my children I do not like to see them starving. We love this country, and we cannot leave it so long as the buffalo are here. The Whites like their country. We do the same and do not want to get rid of it.

"Tell the Great Father to stop the white men from killing the buffalo only for the sake of their hides. So long as there were any buffalo left we were told we might kill them.

"This is all I have to say."

COLONEL DODGE, in reply, informed the Indian Chiefs that he had no instructions to prevent them from hunting buffalo, and, so far as he was aware, they had permission to do so.

"HIGH-BEAR" then made a speech somewhat to the same effect, and informed us that all the buffalo had been driven away from that part of the country by the white hunters; and they believed that the buffaloes were on the head-waters of Republican River. They stated it was a long journey (upwards of 70 miles) without water; and, although they should be very glad to let us see them kill buffalo, they did not advise us to follow them.

October 9th—We breakfasted early, as the Indian Chiefs were to come over to receive the presents. As they did not come the gentlemen were impatient and rode over to see them break camp. About a hundred Indians rode back with them across the river, the Chiefs bringing a note from Mr. Blackmore to the Captain of the escort. They began feeling my riding-habit and braiding. They all wanted to touch me with the ends of their fingers when I came out: the eager curiosity with which they gazed upon me was so funny, looking me all over with a curious smile upon their faces. I do not think they approved of me, generally, but my riding-habit they particularly disapproved, on account of its being tight round the waist. They began in the tent to shake hands with the gentlemen first, but Colonel Dodge pointed to me as the first. They are quite unaccustomed to see any consideration shewn to women: their women never eat with the men; the men eat first and then the women, the children and the dogs. It was an extraordinary sight to see them all move away: they have no wheeled vehicles of any sort; all ride. The babies who are not old enough

to ride are put in baskets: these baskets are firmly tied to two
or three teepee poles, and then the poles are fastened to the
ponies.

We decided to go up the Platte as far as Beaver Creek,
where they say there are numbers of buffalo. The road was a
good one, being the old emigrant-road from the Eastern States
to San Francisco. On the Platte we constantly saw, on the side
of the road, the graves of emigrants who had fallen by the
way, on their march across this Great Desert, as it was called;
for it is only within the last two or three years that people have
discovered the marvellously-nutricious qualities of the buffalo
grass, and have begun to place great herds of cattle upon it
wherever civilization approaches it. We met numbers of
buffalo-hunters, or "Outfits," as they call them. Two or three
men with a waggon and one or two horses make an "Outfit."
They go all over the country killing buffalo, simply for their
hides, which are enormously thick—they say over an inch—
and used for belting in some sorts of machinery. Many of
these men are the roughs of the frontier, criminals flying from
justice, notorious ruffians and murderers, and the settlers are
more afraid of them than of the Indians. We stopped and
spoke to many of them, who all told the stame story, that there
were very few buffalo and double the number of "Outfits" of
any previous year. This looks badly for our prospects of sport.
We heard that large numbers of buffalo were brought in to
Fort Dodge last year, and that the "trail" was lined with a
double row of carcasses for miles: one man had sold 350,000
buffalo hides. It was a charming ride to-day along the banks of
the river. John and Colonel Dodge got several shots at ducks

and wild geese, a peculiar variety, with black wings and white body, and we saw one deer: it was lying in one of the islands in the river, and bounded off with a great many shots after it, but all missed. One of the men killed a badger. An antelope and some jack rabbits were brought in.

There were flocks of starlings on the prairies. We heard wonderful stories of how the starlings will dart down upon the gadflies which settle upon the horses and cattle, and Captain S. says he has seen horses, with two or three starlings perched on their backs, travelling quietly by the side of rivers infested with gadflies. Fortunately for us the mosquitoes and gadflies are over. We had got off so late, on account of the delay with the Indians in the morning, that there was no time for a good hunt. We passed several large ranches: the small low houses attached to a large corral, and surrounded by enormous hayricks. All along the South Platte, within the last few years, these enormous cattle-ranches have been established. One man has a herd of 30,000; they are very profitable. But we passed one ranch in ruins: three years ago it was the scene of a terrible fight with the Indians, and was entirely destroyed. These Indians, until three years ago, had been at perpetual warfare with the Whites and with the other tribes, and only lived by murder and pillage. We have a charming camp on the edge of the river, and I am very glad we are not near those horrid Indians. Some buffalo-hunters have made their camp quite close to us; they say one of them is a most notorious horse-thief and murderer. We are much disgusted with Pallardie, our guide, such a series of lies as he has told us from beginning to end, that we feel we cannot believe a word he says. He is rather sulky this evening, for he feels we do not appreciate him. He made a great push this morning for higher wages, saying to Mr. Blackmore that the Indians wanted him to go with them, and had made him such liberal offers, etc., etc. Mr. Blackmore told him we were quite willing that he should go, we had no desire whatever to keep him, which soon brought him to his senses.

October 10th—I was rather tired this morning, with the three fagging days, so I settled to go in the ambulance along the road by the river, with the escort and waggons, while the gentlemen rode off to the hills in search of buffalo and antelope. They are called hills because the ground everywhere is so flat, but it is only rolling ground. The gentlemen took Pallardie and their orderlies with them; my orderly led my horse behind the ambulance, in case I should want to ride. The day was lovely, clear light Colorado air, and I quite enjoyed the drive, though I was sorry this evening when the others came back that I had not been with them, as they had had a great day's sport, killing a big buffalo and also wolves and antelope. John much disgusted at being defeated by a buffalo calf! The buffalo-hunters they met all say there are no buffalo in Beaver.

The Platte Camp

October 11th—Sunday. We decided to give up Beaver, come back on the Platte camp, where we now are, and hunt over the hills from there: it has been a delicious day for riding, and we saw many wolves. We stopped at a ranche on the way, where we found a pretty young woman who had been married at 14, in Kentucky, and had continued to attend Sunday-School there after her marriage! She was expecting a clergyman to-day to hold a service, but he did not come, and she said she guessed he had been hunting buffalo every Sunday for the last five weeks. The husband of this pretty woman was going to hunt buffalo all the winter, while she went to Denver. All speak of the healthiness of the climate, and the great harm the buffalo-hunters do to settlers, as the buffalo-meat is their principal support for the first few years. We forded the river again and camped on the bank, where we saw rattlesnakes and killed some: belts are made of their skins and earrings of their rattles: I bought some for this purpose.

October 12th—This morning we were off early, to try and find buffalo on the hills. We crossed the river and thought we saw buffalo in the distance on the plain; we rode after them, but they proved to be black cattle. We made for the sand-hills, Pallardie leading: sighted a herd of antelope grazing in a hollow; wolves; quantities of large hawks; more antelope; at last—buffalo! Pallardie stole back: all preparations were made, girths tightened, pistols loaded and carbines. Order of attack was settled; we advanced, buffalo did not move: alas! it was a dead one. We all felt sold, and went on in low spirits; no buffalo to be seen; very down in our luck; buffalo-hunting a delusion and a snare. When we were on the top of a hill, very distant little dark spots were seen moving: glasses instantly

out. Buffalo? yes, buffalo; more come up, a good herd; we
galloped on, keeping as hidden as possible behind small
ridges, until within a half-mile from them: they came in full
view, some lying down, some with calves; we cantered towards them. At first they did not seem to see us; then they
began to move slowly, whereupon we increased our pace;
they broke into a lumbering gallop, faster every moment. The
gentlemen spurred their horses on and endeavoured to plunge
into the herd and separate one from the rest. I remained a
short distance behind, but such a cloud of dust rose that I saw
it all indistinctly. I heard a few shots and I saw through the
dust an animal down, and Pallardie, who was near me, cried
out, "They have killed one"; but, as I galloped up, to my
horror I saw that it was John's horse, stretched out dead, and
John lying partially under him. My first thought was that one
of the others had shot him, but, in a moment, I found that he
was not seriously hurt. His horse had galloped up to the herd
very well, but refused to go amongst them. In trying to urge
him on, John's pistol had gone off, the ball entering the back
of the horse's head; he fell instantly dead, rolling over on
John, but, fortunately, not struggling at all, or John would

certainly have been seriously injured. Mr. Blackmore and one of the soldiers pulled him out immediately; fortunately, he had received no injury, but a hurt in one shoulder, which he declared did not signify. The buffalo, in the meanwhile, had galloped off miles. Just then one of the orderlies cried out, "Why, there's a fellow down," and, looking back we saw, some little distance off, one of the soldiers lying in a heap on the ground, his horse galloping off towards the buffalo. We went to him immediately, and found it was my orderly—Dillon, who seemed very much hurt. His horse had put his foot into a coyote's hole and thrown him violently. He would not let us move him, or hardly touch him, to find out where he was hurt, and he seemed to be in the greatest agony, apparently the spine being injured. After trying carefully for some time to move him, we at last decided we must leave him on the prairie, with a couple of soldiers, and send the ambulance out for him. Of course, the sport for the day was over. My husband was so shaken and his shoulder so painful that he could hardly ride, and, after all these mishaps, the only thing to do was to get back to camp, so we turned our horses' heads toward the Platte, leaving poor Dillon and his two comrades behind us. We were 16 or 18 miles from camp and it seemed very hard leaving them. The ambulance, with Pallardie, could not get back to them before midnight, and Pallardie declared he would have the greatest difficulty in finding them at all, and they must keep good fires on the high places.

We hardly had left them when we discovered another herd of buffalo between us and the camp, but it was so important to get home before dark that we left them and hurried on, send-

ing one of the orderlies in before us to have the ambulance
started, and we met it coming towards us just at sun-down,
and begged Pallardie to get to the men as quickly as possible:
he wanted very much to put it off until the next morning, but
we insisted on his going on. How tired we were! For a moment our spirits revived when, after washing off the dust and
heat, we found a delicious thick soup of buffalo-meat awaiting
us in the cheery mess-tent: but all felt more or less down-
hearted. John's shoulder was so painful he could not move it,
and shooting was at an end for him for several days, at least.
Our forage was exhausted and our horses could not run buffalo. So we decided to make for Sydney as soon as we could.
Rather an inglorious wind-up to an exciting day!

October 13th—At two o'clock last night we heard the ambulance come in. It woke me up by driving over the guy-ropes
which they had fastened to our tent to secure it against the
wind, and I was so glad that they had brought the poor fellow
back so soon. The first thing in the morning, John called out
to know how he was, when we were told that they had not
been able to find him, and had come back to camp to make a
fresh start in the morning. I was sure Pallardie would not go
on, so we settled to go to Riverside Ranch for our camp to-
night, and Pallardie was to bring the men there. I was rather
tired of nothing but game for dinner, and rode up to the ranch
near us before starting, and bought a pair of chickens from
the woman. As we were to have them for dinner that night, I
remembered what Colonel Dodge, who is rather a *gourmet*,
had told me he used to do sometimes to have chickens tender,

and I asked the woman if she had any vinegar. She said, "Yes." So I said, "Will you please give each of the chickens a teaspoonful before you kill them?" I never saw anyone so astonished. What she said was, "Give the chickens vinegar? Wal, now, that beats all. Wal, I declare, you English are a queer people." She was slightly pacified when I told her I was an American, and she was very anxious to induce me to come and settle there: "such a healthy place," she declared. All the people we met on these ranches were so nice and civil and most hospitable. They had all come within the last year or two. A railroad along the Platte is levelled and could, probably, have been laid now had it not been for the financial panic last autumn, which stopped all railroads. We stopped to rest in the middle of the day at quite a new house the man had just bought, where the family had only arrived the day before: they had come down the Platte, and told us that 1,000 Ute warriors had gone into the Republican Valley.

Riverside

October 14th—Camped at Riverside: travelled by compass, shooting antelope. On the prairie every evening one seemed to have slept in the same spot where we had rested the evening before, so exactly alike were our camps on the Platte. The valley of the Platte was 7 or 8 miles wide: for days we had been travelling with hardly any notable change in the scene every day, and yet every day seemed more delightful than the last: there was certainly the charm of great variety of sport, and of the novelty of the little incidents which constantly happened; but, even when we rode, as we sometimes did for hours almost quite silently, there was something exhilarating in the air, in the wonderful sense of freedom, with the vast open expanse in every direction.

October 15th—Left Sydney this morning at seven, the four white mules taking us all to the station so merrily, and looking still so fat, that no one could have believed they had been dragging the ambulance along 30 miles a-day, for the last ten days, over rough prairies and through deep sand-hills, without any forage but what they picked up on the prairie at night. The through train to San Francisco was so crowded that we could not get places in a Palace car, and were obliged to get into one of the general cars, with about 60 people and quantities of children of all ages and every degree of fretfulness from long travelling: poor little things, one could not help feeling sorry for them, but if the Railway would only put on a children's car what a boon it would be. We travelled until one o'clock through the same uninteresting yellow prairie, with low bluffs in the distance and not a tree to be seen, and vast herds of cattle grazing where thousands of buffalo pastured only a year or two ago. This was the worst part of the route for Indian attacks, as the bluffs afforded them a good hiding-place. The train stopped once and we asked why. "Oh, some one was trying to shoot an antelope." We saw a few, and a wolf or two. At Cheyenne we were obliged to stop 12 hours for our train to Denver. Here, to our great astonishment and delight, we came on Colonel Colley.[6] We went into the dining-room to have some food, and there he was! We had heard nothing of him, since we had been together in New York and had made plans for doing the trip together. Somehow, we lost each other, and were so delighted to find him: he goes to Denver with us. He says his California trip is the only mistake of his American tour so far, and the Yosemite did not pay.

John gains a fresh step in military rank every day. He became a Captain on the Mississippi steamboat: at Omaha he was promoted to Major: now no one calls him anything but Colonel. After our life in the open air, the heat of the rooms at the Post last night made me quite faint, and the stoves in the cars to-day were so oppressive. The great discomfort of travel is in the stoves and the cars and the steamboats; the hotels are excellent and clean, and the food is good. We came in sight of the Rocky Mountains this evening, capped with snow.

Denver

October 16th—We were obliged to wait all Friday, the afternoon and evening, at Cheyenne. The Kansas-Pacific Railway has quarrelled with the Union-Pacific, and makes the diabolical arrangement that people must get up at two in the night to go from Cheyenne to Denver, and then no sleeping-car; it was

[6] Afterwards Sir George Pomeroy Colley, killed at Majuba Hill, 1881.

very provoking, for the line runs parallel to the Rocky Mountains and we wanted to see them, besides the discomfort of sitting-up in the uncomfortable seats of the day cars. However, they arranged two seats together for me, and, when the conductor passed, John begged him not to wake me up. I suppose he thought there was something wrong about it, for he poked his lantern under both my seats and all around me. At daybreak I awoke and was well repaid by the exquisite lights of the sunrise on the chain of the Rocky Mountains: it was glorious. The mountains lack the splendid glaciers and wonderful verdure of the Alps, but the outlines of the rocks are bolder and more picturesque. The prairie rolls up to their very feet without a tree, like a sea: and to-day, fortunately, my room is very high up, and the lights and shadows of the masses of clouds hanging over them have been exquisite, doubly beautiful in contrast with the monotony of the prairies we have been living in for a fortnight. We are staying at Charpiot's, a Frenchman who has established a restaurant with a very fair buffet attached: he gave us a delicious breakfast of trout and venison cutlets. The streets are filled with Indians. John went to the Indian Commission, where he found a beautifully-furnished drawing-room and these Indians sitting about, lying on the damask sofas; also in the Bank, with their paint and feathers and bead-work, lodging their money: I saw Ouray, their chief. We drove in the evening to see houses: one was pointed out to me as a "50,000 dollar house." A number of houses are being built. A masquerade ball was going on, and performing animals, but we were too late for the latter. Denver is made by the produce of the mines pouring into it. In the evening Mr. Stevenson came in and told us of his adventures with the Indians, trying to get a photograph of the camp, and how he travels all over the country quite unprotected.

Central City

October 17th—We went by train to-day to Central City—the centre of the gold-mining of this district through the Clear Creek Cañon. Our little train pushed its way near the bed of the Creek right up into the Rocky Mountains,—the rocks rising steeply like castle walls on each side for 600 or 700 feet: for twenty-three miles we turned and twisted around the sharpest curves—every moment disclosing a new view of the most grandly-picturesque description, great masses of rock heaped one on top of the other, sometimes quite overhanging the road, at others sloping-off enough to allow of weird-looking groups of pine trees. We were much amused at the conductor of the train, whose principal occupation seemed to be to find out odd likenesses on the rocks and divert the passengers' attention to them. He would come rushing through the train telling everyone how to "look out up there for the mule with his head down," or to see the head of a man, or "there's the famous old woman with a cap, you see the cap, don't you?" He told me he was a schoolmate of the Governor of Wyoming territory. At Blackhawk we got out of the train and took the omnibus, a mile further up the gorge, to Central City. Every spot of ground where a house could stand was occupied by crushing-

mills, smelting-furnaces and miners' houses, while the hills
above were riddled with holes, gold-mines or "claims." The
gold is found in the quartz, but, as the English manager of one
of the smelting-furnaces told us, they are only as yet scratching
the surface, the deeper they go the richer is the gold deposit:
silver is mixed with it, and great quantities are smelted. John
and Colonel Colley went on the box, and declared the "tallest
swearing" they ever heard issued from the mouth of the
driver at the unfortunate animals he was driving; they were a
very nice team of four horses, but something had put the man
in a bad humour, and, certainly, his manner of driving was
not pleasant. I know, once he started suddenly from a slow
walk up the hill into a furious gallop: the start threw me violently quite flat on the laps of the row of passengers on the
other side, which was anything but pleasant for any of us.
John tried to pacify our Jehu's fury by a little gentle conversation: "How much is a team like this worth here?" "Just
three cents! I wish they'd all lie down and bust their livers."
At the top of the gorge we found a very good hotel, where we
lunched. The hotel was a large new brick building: opposite
it was a small log-house with a large sign— "Mrs. Barnum's
Millinery Store." We then walked through some of the mills;
heaps of gold ore were lying about on the street, and the road
fairly glittered in the sun with bright silver and gold specks.
On the side-walk at one place, we came upon a heap of silver-
bricks still fresh from the furnaces: they were heaped up near
the road entirely unprotected; we heard afterwards they were
worth 28,000 dollars, nearly £6,000. The shops seemed filled
with every luxury for the miners, and I saw beautiful Cali-

fornia fruits for sale. Coming back in the train we sat on an open truck, so that we could better enjoy the beauty of the Cañon, and, certainly, with the evening lights, it was something to remember. Half-way down a party of Chinese were washing the bed of the Creek: they had made a little village, and it was so odd to see the Chinese characters over the shops and the funny little children: and up the steep sides of the Cañon they had terraced little gardens where they grew their vegetables. Everyone speaks of their honesty and trustworthiness, and, though the Irish still hate them, with the rest of the community they seem to be growing more and more popular. When we got to Golden Junction we were put into an odd-looking car, different from the ordinary, and were wondering why it was so, when the conductor came up to us and told us very solemnly, that "President Lincoln's remains had travelled in that car from Washington to his burial place." It was built for him and they had bought it at a bargain from some other Railway Company, and used it, generally, as an excursion car, because it was handy for a band of music in the centre. Found Ouray still hanging about Charpiot's.

Colorado Springs

October 18th—We left Denver this morning for Colorado Springs in the Baby Railway, as they call it, being the first narrow-gauge railway made in this country. It runs South from

Denver skirting the Rocky Mountains, and has opened up the country wonderfully in the last three years. Colorado, it is said, has 365 days of fine weather each year, so that the Pharmacy is unknown. It is so healthy that a man has to be shot, to start a burial-ground. We met some very pleasant people in the train, friends of Mr. Blackmore. We lunched at Colorado Springs and then drove to the garden of the gods. I was not in the least prepared for the wonderful and strange beauties of this freak of nature. The name is most absurd and meaningless, as there is not a flower in it, only red sand-stone shapes; and the view at what is called the "gate" is most peculiar. One drives up the hillside dotted with fir-trees, the red sand-stone rocks contrasting well with the dark green: gradually we came upon rocks standing-out from the others in most extraordinary shapes, and of the deepest red colours, shaded sometimes very much lighter. These fantastic forms became larger and larger until we reached the gates—two enormous rocks standing opposite to each other and rising nearly perpendicularly on each side, forming a passage through by the centre. As we looked through them at the mountains rising one over the other in the splendid evening light and shade, and crowned by "Pike's Peak" covered with snow, I thought I had never seen anything so beautiful. It was worth coming 7,000 miles to see. We then came on two miles to this little watering-place which has sprung up in the last two years, on our way passing the very pretty house built by Dr. Bell, author of that delightful book which first revealed to us the wonders of the great Cañons. He was so pleased with this part of America, that he has brought his wife over and they have made their home in this charming spot. We are staying at a new hotel just built and very comfortable.

The Springs are soda, but the air is the great specific, and persons with delicate chests are here for the winter. Though it is 7,000 feet above the sea, and amongst the mountains, it is never very cold and the air is so dry that it has worked wonders. A number of young Englishmen have come out to take ranches for cattle.

Attached to this house is a very nice restauarant kept by a Frenchman, and called the *maison dorée*. The food was very good, all but some chickens which had been killed an hour before dinner, without having their dose of vinegar, and, being hardy mountaineers with their muscles well developed, were impossible. The proprietress of this hotel is a very nice English lady, who only took possession of it two months ago, the house itself only being begun in June, and yet now quite dry and comfortable. It was so pleasant to sit in the cosy drawing-room, which looked like a little bit of England, after all our roughing it, and the springs are like delicious soda-water.

October 19th—John and Colonel Colley ascended Pike's Peak to-day: it is about 14,000 feet above the sea and 8,000 above this, and the ascent is an easy one, on horseback nearly the whole way. There was a little snow on the upper part, and an observatory with a telegraph attached: three men are kept there, being changed once a year—a dull life. The view is very grand, on one side over the Rocky Mountains, on the other over the prairie, where some rain-storms crossed. A man was lost on Pike's Peak the other day for 48 hours; he got separated from his party in a fog, and fell over a precipice on to a small plateau. His friends came back to Manitou after searching in vain for him, and told his wife of his disappearance. She at once made up her mind she would never see him again, and packed up all her things and his and returned to the East by the first train. The next day a party went out to search for him, and, after a long search, he was found, lifted up from the plateau and brought back, very much bruised and knocked about and intensely disgusted to find his wife and his clothes were all gone. They saw numbers of mountain squirrels on the top of Pike's Peak: I had seen some in Denver which I longed to bring home.

I luxuriated in a quiet morning, mended my tattered garments, and looked over Dr. Bell's book: and Dr. and Mrs. Bell came to see me and asked us all to dine in the evening. In the afternoon Mr. Blackmore drove me to Glen Eyrie—General Palmer's place. We drove through the garden of the gods, which again filled me with admiration. The same wonderful rocks are scattered over General Palmer's place and are of such startling contrast of colours; in one place an immense jagged table-like rock rises over 100 feet high of the brightest-red colour; and close to it another rock quite as large of the same shape, but a light-grey colour, curiously marked with large patches of bronze, green and bright-brown. If these scenes were painted and exhibited in England, they would be so startling and sensational, that no one would believe for an instant that they could be true to nature. We wanted to visit Monument Park, about ten miles off, where the grey rocks form themselves into castles, cathedrals, etc., but we had not time. We also heard a great deal of the Cañon of the Arkansas River, near Cañon City, which we had intended to go and see. It is a deep cleft in the rock, 2,000 feet deep and about 12 miles long.

Denver

October 20th—We decided this morning to give up any further excursions, and to turn our faces Eastward, so as to endeavour to catch the *Cuba* on the 28th. I am very sorry not to explore further these wonderful mountains and the Parks that lie in them—a month could be well spent. For the first time since we have left New York we to-day retraced our steps, from Manitou here. But to-morrow we again take a new line —the Kansas-Pacific will be all new ground. We have telegraphed for a drawing-room compartment.

October 21st—To-day we turned our faces Eastward once more. Rain fell at night, as if we had ordered it specially to lay the dust. Fog in the morning, but, although the thermometer was 40°, one hardly felt cold: the usual lot of unhealthy cadaverous-looking people swarming around the hotel stove. The hotel people had us up an hour too soon (they treat one like children always) and sent us off to the train too early— one can never have the pleasure of being just in time. The weather cleared up, to an exquisite Indian-summer haze, which softened the endless horizon of yellow prairie, and I found the day so enjoyable, now sitting quietly in my comfortable little drawing-room reading some *Times* that had reached us at Denver; now, on a camp-stool on the platform at the back of the carriage enjoying the delicious air, so exquisitely light and pure. We passed any number of herds of antelope, and, as for the prairie-dogs, we went through several of their towns, lasting for miles: the impertinent little creatures do not mind the train in the least, and it does not even excite them enough to make them wag their tails: they were so close that we could see the expressions of their upturned faces: they stood on their hind-legs with their front-paws scratching their noses and giving us an occasional glance. In riding over the prairie one hardly saw anything of them but a rush and a furious wag of the tail before they dived into their holes. Some of my friends tried to persuade me to take a pair of prairie-dogs home with me as pets, but they will burrow through almost anything, which is a bother sometimes. After I had heard the experiences of a gentleman who had taken two home with him to tame, I was very glad that I had given up the idea. This gentleman had them in a cage with a wooden bottom. They went on very well for a few days, but, one night at an hotel where he was staying, they burrowed and scratched a hole through the floor of the cage, then through the floor of the room: then they ran along between the joists to the corner of the next room, where they began burrowing upwards. A lady's trunk was standing in the corner, and they actually scratched and gnawed until they had made a hole in the floor and the bottom of the trunk, and then the little wretches worked their way up through all the unfortunate lady's clothes, and came out at the top of the trunk! ! ! How these little creatures live and grow round and fat, as they do, is a marvel, for one never sees them more than a few yards from their holes, and the ground is quite bare. Our car is heated with hot-water and with the ventilators open is perfect. John has just been through the rest of the train and says the ordinary cars are Tophet.

Kansas

October 22nd—When we awoke this morning we had left the dry and endless prairie, and were going through pretty woods by the side of a broad river; it was so refreshing. We were in the State of Kansas—bleeding Kansas, shrieking Kansas, as it used to be known. It was in the struggle to take slavery into this State that feelings became so embittered between the North and South, and I remember the time when Kansas was perpetually shrieking for freedom, slaves were brought-in in gangs, and there were fights and bloodshed: now the comfortable homesteads we passed looked peaceful enough. It is impossible to describe the exquisite beauty of autumn in spots like these: the gorgeous colours of the foliage would be too dazzling, were it not for the dreamy haze of the Indian summer, which mellows the splendour of these vivid reds and yellows.

We passed through the Kaw Valley, where great attempts were made to civilize the Kaw Indians: they were a large tribe and possessed this beautiful rich country. The Methodist Mission devoted themselves to this work of civilizing and Christianising them: immense sums of money were raised, nice little houses were built for them, but all in vain. They put their ponies in the houses and lived themselves in their tents, the doors and woodwork they tore down for firewood, and the little boys made targets of the window-panes for their bows and arrows. The tribe is now nearly extinct. All authorities will tell you that it is as impossible to civilize them as to tame a wolf. These men will not work: when you shake hands with them their long fingers feel just like the paw of an animal, with a softness like hair. In California and the West, families have often tried to take young children and bring them up to civilization, but, after the age of ten or twelve, it is impossible to do anything with them. One lady had a pretty little girl who had lived with her for several years, and she had taken great pains with her. This lady was also fond of canary-birds and reared quantitites of them, but a number disappeared in a most unaccountable manner. One day she noticed two tiny little yellow feathers sticking to the corner of the little Indian girl's mouth. She watched her, and found the little wild thing used to catch the canary-birds in their cage and eat them alive!

October 23rd—At Topeka we changed trains, and, to my dismay, there was only one drawing-room compartment in the Pullman car we took to St. Louis, and that was engaged by a young couple who had been married that morning, so I was obliged to resign myself to a section which is not at all nice for ladies; one's bed is curtained-in, but to stand on a spring and to dress and undress, with the carriage swaying about, is a most heart-breaking proceeding, and there was the difficulty of washing! I did see ladies with their hair down and in their dressing-gowns walk quietly down the centre of the car from their section to the wash-room, through rows of half-dressed men, but I could not; and I was very miserable because I had not my nice little dressing-room attached to the drawing-room compartment. Soon after leaving Topeka our train stopped at a small station and took in a horde of the most dreadful people, noisy politicians who had been at a "Barbecue," a great political meeting of some sort. A few of them had the sections opposite to mine, and kept up their political rant until long after everyone had gone to bed: the gentle language and mild oaths that they used in reference to the opposition candidates were edifying! I went to sleep in the middle of it.

St. Louis

We arrived at St. Louis at 6 in the morning, breakfasted, and crossed the Mississippi River on the great bridge, in an omnibus, to take the Vandalia line to Indianopolis. The trains have not yet run across the bridge, though it is quite finished. We found no delightful Pullman attached to our train, and were obliged to travel until 4 o'clock in one of the ordinary cars, which was more detestable than usual, being crowded with families of settlers who had been trying their fortunes in vain at the West, and were returning to their friends in the East.

Every autumn sees this tide of returning emigration—generally ne'er-do-wells—who go from one place to another and never succeed anywhere; but this autumn more than usual are returning on account of the distress amongst the Western Settlers, caused by the grass-hoppers and the drought. But wherever one travels in America this extraordinary restlessness of the people strikes one. Whole families move hither and thither in every direction, trying first one thing and then another until they meet fortune in some shape. One could not help pitying these poor people in the train to-day, though they made one very uncomfortable. Most of them had come great distances, travelling for days in the cheap cars without going to bed or resting. The poor weary mothers seemed worn out in looking after cross, fretful, tired-out children; and the disappointed, disheartened-looking men, seemed only to have energy enough left to chew tobacco and spit incessantly! And all, oh! so unwashed! It was a beautiful mild day, but a great stove roared in the corner of the car, and with the greatest difficulty I managed to keep a window open next to my seat: we were greatly overcrowded. I am sorry to say our struggles for fresh air have had a most demoralizing effect upon John's veracity. He began by little fibs, such as "the lady is not very well," but was soon hardened in his career, and such little scenes as the following have been of daily occurrence:—"I say, Mister, will you shut that window, please, we are most froze over here?" John: "I am very sorry but this lady is suffering from asthma, and it is absolutely necessary she should have fresh air." "Look here, stranger, we can't stand that window any longer, it'll give us all consumption, sure." John:

"I regret to say this lady is threatened with a fit, and I can't say what may be the consequences if the window is shut." I certainly had a fit after this last overwhelming assertion, but to-day he surpassed himself. The seats were so cramped that we kept an extra one and I put my feet on it. Very soon some people came in and requested us to "turn out of that, please." But John was equal to the occasion: "Sir, I am sorry to say this lady is suffering from a bad leg, and it is very important for her to keep her feet up." Asthma and fits I could stand, but a "bad leg" was *too* much, and I did not insist upon keeping my extra seat. We passed through a most lovely country—a part of Southern Illinois and Indiana, beautifully-wooded knolls and banks and valleys, where the richest crops were growing, but I noticed very few farm-houses, only a miserable shanty here and there: and we were told that the malaria was so frightful that it was impossible to live there, the owners came near it only to put in their crops and gather them. At Terre Haute we came upon ironworks and passed coalmines continually during the day. The air felt so dull and heavy in contrast to the exhilarating lightness of that we had been breathing on the prairie and Rocky Mountains. At four o'clock, at Indianopolis, we again changed cars, and I was delighted to find myself again in a comfortable little drawing-room compartment, for which we had telegraphed. We met an American officer in the train, who had been stationed for three years in Arizona, and had now six months' leave of absence. Of all the frontier stations those in Arizona are the worst, completely isolated, the heat terrible, averaging 110° in the shade all the summer; it is complete banishment to an educated person. He told me their only amusement was a small pack of hounds they had established to hunt jack-rabbit, which is really a large hare.

October 24th—I slept so well last night, and John got up quite melancholy that this was our last night in the cars! We breakfasted at Pittsburg, and then got into one of "Pullman's Day Palace Cars," divided into three rooms, with rows of easy chairs and sofas. Our route is the same as that we came over on leaving New York, but we passed through most of it during the night. Now with this autumn colouring on the hills it seems most beautiful—and perfect comfort, after our first contest for windows open, as we glide smoothly and swiftly along at about the same rate as the first-half of the day—scenery first wild,—then by the rich farmyards of Pennsylvania, celebrated for their wonderful barns, the lower storey for cows and stock, the second for horses, and then three or four stories for storage, showily painted, and on one I saw a weathercock—a gilt horse the size of life.

New York

October 25th—We found our kind host last night sitting up to receive us. How I wish I could properly describe him, his kind benevolent face with his long white hair, his bright intelligent dark eyes, telling how keen his intellect is still, in spite of his 84 years; every new discovery in science and mechanics he watches with as much interest as if he was just

Grandmamma

entering life. It was a delicious day of rest. I read an accumulation of letters and delightful home news. Settled to sail on Wednesday in the *Cuba*.

October 26th—This morning John and I went over to Staten Island, to see Mrs. Bury and enquire about poor Lord Charleville, who is dying of consumption. Mr. Duncan has lent them his place. The day was beautiful and bright, and, from the porch, the views of New York bay, quite blue and covered with white sails, framed in the brilliant reds and yellows of the oaks and maples, resplendent in the bright sunlight; the world looked so enjoyable, the air so clear and as if throbbing with life; it seemed a glory to live, and too hard to think of that young life ebbing away in the midst of it all. I saw Mrs. Bury for a few moments. The contrast of the melancholy inside and nature's festival outside was almost shocking and very depressing. In the evening John went to some political meeting with Mr. Hewitt; he is "running for Congress," and his house is besieged with what they call "Strikers"—men who want money for their votes, not an unheard-of-creature in England, but here they ask for it more openly. Mr. Hewitt is determined not to give it to them, and I am afraid the opposite candidate will be successful, as he has no such scruples. His opponent belongs to the same party, but is a low butcher and gambler; the voters are principally Irish.

October 27th—Very busy all day, doing some shopping: got a lot of "Piazza chairs," a sort of wickerwork which will stand any amount of weather, and the only kind which I find do not go to pieces from the damp of the Winter Garden at home; also some driving-whips made of malacca-cane and gutta-percha, very long and very light. I used to take back barrels of American apples and canned fruit, until I found that, like nearly everything else, with much less trouble I could get the very same things, just as good and a great deal cheaper, in London. In the evening we had a farewell dinner at the Coopers'.

The Cuba

October 28th—Again on the *Cuba* with Captain Martyn. We had to be on board at seven in the morning on account of the tide. The *Adriatic*, of the White Star line, left the harbour at the same time as we did, and it was rather provoking to think how much sooner she would arrive in Queenstown. She is very fast and the *Cuba* rather the reverse; besides, the Cunarders go 100 miles to the South now, so as to avoid collisions. They have had a wonderful reputation for safety, never having lost a ship, so that they rather presume upon it. The weather is lovely, the wind fair behind us, the *Adriatic* steaming away nearly out of sight in front. The ship was so full that we have been obliged to take one of the officers' cabins on deck: it is very comfortable and Tom Jones, the steward, has arranged all my things as if he had been a lady's maid all his life; and, if things become very bad, I must depend on him, for the stewardess—not my dear Mrs. ———, but a stern-looking lady with a black wig—has informed me that she never goes upstairs.

November 2nd—So far we have had a perfectly smooth sail, a fair wind and the weather almost too hot. Our Captain is perfection—so agreeable, having been in almost every part of the world, and able and willing to talk, and so devoted to his profession and so clever in it, as all testify. We have some very pleasant fellow-passengers: a clever doctor, and an ex-private-secretary, pleasant and clever but belonging to that tiresome school of Radicals, who are more bigoted in their own ideas for the regeneration of England, and more narrow-minded than the most inveterate Tory of the old school. Tom Jones has kept up his character for care and civility, even to sewing buttons on my boots; he neglects nothing which is all the more admirable, as I know, in his heart, he disapproves of a lady occupying one of these rooms.

November 4th—Yesterday morning the wind freshened into a very stiff gale, as we thought it; unfortunately, there is a barometer in our room, and, as we watched it steadily going down all the morning, we abandoned ourselves to the most gloomy anticipations, and the sea washed over the deck so constantly that I could not get out of my room: but the faithful Tom Jones braved everything and kept us supplied with the necessaries of life. In spite of the barometer the afternoon got better and I went in to dinner, when the Captain tried to explain to me that it is "perfectly useless looking at a barometer, without you understand it," and that I did not understand it at all; but it seems to me all Captains on these boats have the same sort of idea about passengers—a passenger is an inferior animal who comes on board with its easy chair and asks silly questions; it must be treated gently, but with firmness, and kept at a distance, and any notion that it may have picked up from observation—about the ship's going too slow—economy of coals—rotten sails, etc.—must be nipped in the bud and treated with the greatest contempt. Our Captain, who in every other way is charming, was constantly beginning a sentence such as, " 'Pon my word, passengers are ———," or, "Well, really, it is inconceivable how passengers do ———." Out of consideration for our small feelings he never quite committed himself, but there is a shake of the head and a turn of the brow that makes us feel keenly what miserable creatures we are.

The day being showery, John has been explaining the Irish Land Act to the Governor of Colorado territory, who is going to realize "the dream of his life," and visit Europe. He is filled with astonishment that such a revolutionary measure could have been passed in England, indeed, no intelligent American can understand the English Government deliberately doing such an act of injustice to any class as that Act did to the Irish landlords.

The day was so rough that the bride of 16, whose husband announced to the Captain that she was fit to be a sailor's wife, has collapsed, but the fair one with the golden locks (aureoline) and her dark-haired companion are still there; she has announced that her object in going to Europe is to get up a Company to work some wonderful mines in California: her husband is obliged to remain there to look after them.

FINIS